Christ and the Crowds

James E. Carter

Broadman Press
Nashville, Tennessee

© Copyright 1981 • Broadman Press
All rights reserved.

4251-81
ISBN: 0-8054-5181-1

Dewey Decimal Classification: 232.9
Subject heading: JESUS CHRIST

Library of Congress Catalog Card Number: 80-68467
Printed in the United States of America

All Scripture quotations are from the King James Version of the Bible unless otherwise noted.

Scripture quotations marked (NEB) are from *The New English Bible.* Copyright © The Delegates of the Oxford University Press and the Syndics of the Cambridge University Press, 1961, 1970. Reprinted by permission.

Scripture quotations marked (Phillips) are reprinted with the permission of Macmillan Publishing Co., Inc. from J. B. Phillips: *The New Testament in Modern English,* Revised Edition. © J. B. Phillips 1958, 1960, 1972.

Scripture quotations marked (RSV) are from the Revised Standard Version of the Bible, copyright 1946, 1952, © 1971, 1973.

To the life and memory of
CAROLYN LEE
Who emerged from out of the crowd as a
superior secretary
faithful friend
consistent Christian

Foreword

A former president instructed his wife, "Walk slowly through the crowds." Jesus always walked slowly through the crowds. Individuals in the group always drew his attention.

Crowds were always with Jesus. From his birth to his death, he was in a crowd. This study is an attempt to examine some of the faces Jesus pulled out of the various crowds at specific times in his life.

Obviously, it will not deal with all of the people whom Jesus met and to whom he ministered. But it will deal with some representative people at representative times and places in the ministry of the Master.

From the crowds of people I have known and with whom I have shared life and ministry, I must express appreciation to the University Baptist Church, Fort Worth, Texas, for the freedom to write the book; to Betty Hatcher, veteran and faithful pastor's secretary at University Baptist Church for assistance in preparing the manuscript; and to my family for the encouragement to write.

Christ singled individuals out of the crowd for his attention and love. I trust that individuals will continue to find help, enlightenment, and strength through this work from the Christ who walked slowly through the crowds.

JAMES E. CARTER

Contents

Part I: The Crowd at the Cradle
1. Mary: Preparing for His Coming........... 7
2. Herod: Protecting His Own Life 16
3. Innkeeper: Providing for His Birth 23
4. Shepherds: Preserving His Presence 30

Part II: The Crowd in the Country
5. The Gadarene Demoniac: When Evil Is Destroyed 38
6. The Rich, Young Ruler: When Life Is Explained 46
7. The Paralytic: When Ministry Is Performed.. 54
8. The Syro-Phoenician Woman: When Faith Is Demonstrated...................... 60

Part III: The Crowd in the City
9. A Crippled Man: The Compassion of Christ . 70
10. A Blind Man: The Light from Christ........ 77
11. A Lawyer: The Commandment to Love 84
12. Mary of Bethany: The Extravagance of Love. 91

Part IV: The Crowd at the Cross
13. Priests: The Resisting of Reality............ 99
14. Simon of Cyrene: The Involvement of Bystanders 106
15. Centurion: The Confession of Christ 112
16. The Marys: The Transformation of Tragedy . 120
    Afterword............................. 127

Part I
The Crowd at the Cradle

Jesus was even born in a crowd. Around the familiar Christmas story crowd a number of persons. To each of them Christ had a particular meaning and a special relationship.

1

Mary: Preparing for His Coming

We had just come out of the Greek Orthodox Church of the Annunciation in Nazareth. The church is built directly over Mary's well, the traditional place where the angel appeared to Mary to announce the coming birth of Jesus. It is fairly authentic since it is the only water source in old Nazareth. It still has water. Once Turkish conquerors rode their horses into the church to water them. After that the water was piped out to a well on the street a little way from the church.

The guide at the church was upset. After his explanation of the event and the place, we went to the altar then viewed the well through a grate. As we left, he asked for tips and tried to sell slides and picture postcards. Since an adequate tip had been given already for the group, individuals had been told there was no need to tip him again. The slides did not sell well to our group either. When we left, I saw the guide slam down his packages of slides and utter angry words at us because we had not been more profitable to him.

What a tragedy, I thought. *Here is a Christian and a church who have entirely forgotten their purpose. Their purpose is to tell the story of the birth of Jesus and its meaning to the world. Here the preparation was made for the presence of the Christ in the world. Now all energy and effort is put into protecting a place, in protecting a place whose purpose has been forgotten.*

In preparing for the coming of Jesus into our world, we have to go back, at least mentally, to that place and to that person to whom the announcement was first given: Mary of Nazareth. Mary is the first and most obvious person in the crowd at the cradle when Jesus came into this world.

Mary has hardly been treated fairly by Christians. Roman

Catholics have given too much attention to her; other Christians have given too little attention to her. Obviously, she was a person of good character and strong faith. She was probably a teenager. According to some traditions, her mother had died and she had two younger sisters at home. If this were true, she likely served as the mistress of the home and was no stranger to responsibility. Traditionally, the well at Nazareth has been considered the spot for the encounter with the angel, although the account in Luke 1:26-38 does not mention the site. Out of all the chosen people, God chose this girl to be the mother of his Son. Mary prepared for Jesus' coming.

Notice where the announcement was made. It was not shouted from the heavens; it was whispered to a girl. It was not given even in the center of the Promised Land; it was given in Galilee, called Galilee of the Gentiles because of its high Gentile population. The announcement was not proclaimed in Jerusalem, the city of worship; it was told in Nazareth, a place so indistinguished that an early disciple could say, "Can anything good come out of Nazareth?" (John 1:46, RSV). It was not published in the Temple, where the religious had prayed for centuries for such an announcement; it was quietly given in a simple place, perhaps even a public place. One out of the crowd at the cradle had prepared for Jesus' coming in a particularly significant way.

A People

Mary was a Jewess, one of God's chosen people. In a unique way, God had prepared a people to receive his Son.

Someone has said that nothing is ever universal until it is first local. In a real way this is true with the incarnation. For Jesus to be the Savior of humankind, he had to become a person in a local community born into a particular family.

When analyzing Mary's reaction to the angelic announcement, notice that Mary was more surprised at the content of the announcement than she was at the visit of the angel. As a Jewess, she was a part of a people who were accustomed to dealing with God. She believed in angels. To think that an angel would appear to a mere human with a message from God was not difficult for Mary to accept. The substance of the message—that she was to be the virgin mother of the Promised One of God—was more difficult to accept.

Running through the announcement of the angel are several streams of words from the prophets. These prophets had helped the people believe that God would send his Messiah, the Promised One, to them at some time in some way. God would act, and he would act decisively.

A Person

God had also prepared a person for the coming of Christ. Mary was prepared by God for her specific task. Even with the prophetic preparation, few people actually expected God to enter the human race—and certainly not through a Jewish peasant girl! Likely the little girls of Palestine did not play games wondering who would be the mother of the Messiah.

The angel said to Mary, "Hail, thou that art highly favoured, the Lord is with thee: blessed art thou among women" (Luke 1:28). The Revised Standard Version translates it more simply, "Hail, O favored one, the Lord is with you!" (Luke 1:28). Surely Mary was the most blessed among women. The most blessed thing a Jewish woman could consider was to be the mother of the Messiah.

The expression, "The Lord is with thee," is really about all that we need to know about Mary. We do not have any reason to believe that she was sinlessly perfect, immaculately conceived, or perpetually a virgin. But we do believe that in preparing Mary for a specific purpose God was with her. God's favor did not rest in unbroken happiness, ease, pleasure, or prosperity.

Life is not to be lived solely for oneself. Life is to be shared with others. When God chooses a person for a task, God prepares the person for that task. Your task may not be as glorious as giving birth to the Savior of the world, but there are no little jobs in God's service.

Around Christmas every year, our denomination is reminded of a woman who refused to live for self. Lottie Moon, for whom the "Lottie Moon Christmas Offering for Foreign Missions" was named, was appointed in 1873 as a missionary to China. For nearly forty years, she served the cause of Christ, skipping furloughs and sharing her resources with starving Chinese. She died on Christmas Eve, 1924, on board ship in the harbor of Kobe, Japan, on the way home. In 1888, she first suggested a special offering at Christmas for foreign missions. A person prepared by God for a task inspired other people who had been touched by God in their task of Christian missions.

Note that preparation to do God's will goes on with little awareness on the part of the individual that he is being prepared for God's service. Mary had no way of knowing that she was being prepared to be the mother of Jesus. She had no way of knowing prior to the announcement by the angel that she was blessed by God in this unique way. God was at work in Mary's life while she lived her life in what seemed to her to be natural expressions of growth and service.

Johnny Cash, the well-known country and western singer, suffered a marriage failure as well as moral and emotional problems. His pastor played a big part in Cash's rehabilitation. In a "This Is Your Life" television program, the minister related that he had heard Johnny Cash sing on the radio and determined that he would look Cash up, get acquainted with him, and offer to him the services of the congregation and the minister. Cash's response was positive. That pastor and that church helped Cash move back toward a happy and productive life.

The pastor related that he offered to help Cash because famous young men need love too. The pastor was not a particularly impressive person; his church was not a well-known church related to a major demonination. Likely, he was not aware that he was being prepared to play a major role in the reclamation of a well-known entertainer; but he was.

Purpose

There was a purpose in the preparation for the coming of Christ. The purpose of Jesus' coming was expressed to both Joseph (Matt. 1:20) and to Mary:

MARY

> He will be great, and will be called the Son
> of the Most High;
> and the Lord God will give to him the
> throne of his father David,
> and he will reign over the house of Jacob
> for ever;
> and of his kingdom there will be no end
> (Luke 1:32-33, RSV).

Jesus' purpose was in his name. The name *Jesus* is the Greek form of the Hebrew name *Joshua.* The name means "the salvation of God." When the name Jesus is repeated, the purpose of God is expressed: the salvation of God. Jesus was to come into the world to bring the salvation of God to people in need of salvation. What's in a name? Salvation is in that name.

God will be with us. Emmanuel is another name given to Jesus. It means "God with us." With the coming of Christ into our world, we have the visual reminder that God is with us.

The descriptions of Jesus given to Mary show that God is with us in Jesus Christ. He is great. He is the Son of God. In a unique way that we can neither understand nor explain, he is the virgin-born Son of God. In Jesus Christ, God is with us in a special way. What hope this gives us in seemingly hopeless situations. We are not without hope: God is with us. And what reassurance this gives us. We have the presence of Christ with us. We are not alone.

Just before Easter, 1980, an elderly woman called the office of the Fort Worth (Texas) *Star-Telegram* from a hospital room. In a forty-five minute conversation with a reporter in the newspaper office, the woman revealed that she was eighty-one years old, that her husband and son were both dead, that she had no living relatives, and that she just wanted to tell someone good-bye before she died. After detailing her life, she indicated that she was not disillusioned or bitter about life; she just wanted to tell someone good-bye. She never did say who she was or where she was. She said good-bye. She was still alone, but she seemed satisfied.

The newspaper was swamped with calls the day the story about the woman was run. Older people, who were in similar situations, and younger people, who missed grandparents or who were separated from their parents, called wanting to know how to get in touch with the woman. They were willing to talk with her. They wanted to share her life and to help relieve her loneliness. With Christ in our world, we are never alone. At no time and at no place do we face life by ourselves. God is with us.

Jesus will reign forever. That kingdom will never end. This is seen in God's purpose. The promise of God to David that his house would rule forever was to be fulfilled ultimately in Jesus Christ. Those who looked for the Messiah to restore the kingdom of Israel were to be disappointed politically. But all who look to the reign of God in the hearts of humans are satisfied spiritually. This Jesus, the Promised One of God, will reign eternally. Jesus founded a spiritual kingdom that never ends.

Queen Victoria of England once remarked that she wanted to lay her crown at Jesus' feet. Her kingdom was temporal and limited. His kingdom was spiritual and eternal.

Possibility

A possibility is highlighted in the preparation for Jesus' coming. The possibility is that nothing is impossible with God, even our redemption from sin.

Mary's response was one of wonder. She took the angel's word seriously and wondered how she would bear this promised Child since she was not married. This promise seemed unlikely to be fulfilled by Mary because she was still a virgin. The question of how the virgin birth might be possible is not a new question. It was first asked by Mary, herself.

The answer is that the virgin birth was possible because of the power of God. Through the overshadowing of the Holy Spirit, the act was done by the power of God. It was God's act. Don't get too physical and crass here. We are treading on the ground of mystery and wonder. Too detailed explanations can remove the majesty of the mystery.

We know that God gave himself to an earthly, human origin. The incarnation has something to do with God's continuing relationship with the universe. To be a man he had to have flesh. To have flesh he had to be born of a woman. God became incarnate through the birth of Jesus by the virgin Mary. What a fascinating and fantastic possibility that is! God became one of us; he was willing to share life with us. As Frederick B. Speakman expressed it, God dared to take his own medicine by living in this world. But the incarnation was possible only through the power of God.

The most beautiful expression in the annunciation is Mary's expression of submission to the will of God: "Behold, I am the handmaid of the Lord; let it be to me according to your word" (Luke 1:38, RSV). Mary was willing for God's will to be done in her life whether she understood it or not. Since she was the handmaid of the Lord, one who was dedicated to him and willing to serve him, she was ready to serve him in whatever way he asked. As William Barclay commented, Mary had learned to forget the world's commonest prayer, Thy will be changed, and had learned to pray the world's greatest prayer, Thy will be done.

What does God demand of us? Commitment to him and to his will is the demand of God. A seminary professor tells of coming home as a college ministerial student to find his widowed mother carefully figuring her tithe. He was a bit shocked at her legalism as she meticulously multiplied her weekly salary by 10 percent and then placed that exact amount in her envelope. But before he could protest what appeared to him to be a crass, narrow-minded cheapening of grace, his mother took out a second envelope from the drawer and placed a bill or two in it. Then she explained that she gave her tithe because she knew she should; the other envelope was the extra that she gave because she wanted to give. Fortunately he had not spoken and did not for several moments. There was nothing he could add to her understanding of commitment and stewardship.

Nothing is impossible with God! That is more than an angelic assertion (Luke 1:37). It is also a positive reality. With God it was possible for a virgin girl to bear a son who is the Son of God. With God it was possible for an older barren woman to bear a son who was the forerunner for the Son of God. The news of Elizabeth's pregnancy was given to Mary as a proof of the power of God (Luke 1:36). With God, persons can find redemption in Christ and have new life through faith in him.

Solomon Ginsburg was the son of a Jewish rabbi. When he was thirteen years old, he asked a question in a discussion of the rabbis who had come to help his father celebrate the Feast of the Tabernacles. The question he asked concerned Isaiah 53. He wanted to know to whom the prophet referred. Repeating the question when he thought he was not heard, his father slapped him and angrily left the room.

Two years later Ginsburg was in London working for an uncle. On Whitechapel Street, he met a Jewish Christian missionary. The missionary invited Ginsburg to a mission to hear a sermon on Isaiah 53. When the missionary asked Ginsburg if he believed following the sermon, he replied that he did not know and explained that his father was a rabbi. The missionary told him to read the New Testament and then ask himself if Jesus is the Messiah predicted in Isaiah 53.

This Ginsburg did. He became convinced when he read the crucifixion account and the words of Matthew 27:25, "His blood be on us, and on our children." Ginsburg struggled for three months with the decision to become a Christian. He finally confessed faith in Christ.

Ginsburg's uncle discharged him and put him out on the street with only the clothes that he wore. The family disowned and disinherited him.

Even though his family had turned their backs on him, Ginsburg did not turn his back on his newfound Messiah. He went to college. Then he went to Brazil as a missionary in 1890. During his years of ministry there, despite persecution which even included imprisonment, he saw Baptists grow from less than a thousand to more than twenty-one thousand. With God nothing is impossible.

MARY

Jesus Christ came into our world. Preparing for his coming was a Jewish girl named Mary. She was certainly one of the crowd at the cradle. She was peculiarly prepared by God to prepare for Jesus' coming. She was his mother.

2

Herod: Protecting His Own Life

A well-known novelist once shared a question that was asked her by a beautiful and intelligent Polish girl who had married an American. On her first Christmas in America, the Polish girl asked why Americans celebrated the feast of Saint Nicholas and the birth of Christ on the same day. She did not feel that was possible. The feast of Saint Nicholas, she said, was a celebration of things. It was a family day. There were decorated trees, stockings, presents, and food. She asked what that had to do with the birth of the Christ in a poor manger to be the Savior of the world.

How do you relate Christmas as both a holy day and a holiday? The Polish girl said that in her country they celebrate on two days: Saint Nicholas' Day presents are given and festivities are enjoyed, and Christmas Day is a day of worship.

The novelist struggled to explain why Christmas in America is a celebration of both a holy day and a holiday. Then she remembered that she had seen the two combined in a way that brought tears to her eyes. Her granddaughter was seven or eight years of age and was just learning to cook. She had baked a small round cake with white icing and was placing a large red candle right in the middle of it as the novelist came down to Christmas Eve dinner. The granddaughter explained with a smile that the Baby Jesus ought to have a birthday cake on his birthday. Nobody seemed to remember that, so she had made him one herself. She lighted the candle and sang happy birthday to Baby Jesus. Since then they have had a birthday cake for Jesus at their family Christmas dinner. It is their way of combining the two meanings of Christmas. It is their attempt to protect Christmas.

One of the biggest problems Christians always have around

HEROD

Christmas is trying to protect Christmas from encroachments into its Christian meaning. When we join the crowd around the cradle at the birth of Jesus, we want to remember that birth for its spiritual significance. But it gets difficult. Interestingly enough, protecting Christmas has always been a difficulty.

Only Matthew records the story of the visit of the Magi, the Wise Men, to the baby Jesus (2:1-13). While searching for the birthplace of the new King, the Wise Men stopped by the palace of King Herod. Feigning interest, Herod asked when they had first seen the star; this would help him determine the age of the Child. Then he asked the Wise Men to return to tell him where the Child was in order to worship him himself. Actually, Herod was more interested in killing him than in worshiping him. Warned in a dream, the Wise Men returned home by another route.

But Herod would take no chances. Computing the probable age of the Child from the time the Magi had first seen the star, Herod killed all the boy babies under two years of age born in Bethlehem. This shows that the Magi were some time in getting to Bethlehem.

Shortly after the birth of Christ, Mary and Joseph fled to Egypt to protect the Christ from the wrath of Herod (Matt. 2:13-15). Matthew found a prophecy to fit the flight to safety.

Herod seems a strange figure to draw out from the crowd at the cradle. His presence there was incidental at best. But he represents, from a negative standpoint, how we must protect the Christ. Herod, who tried to eliminate the Christ, shows us how we can protect Christmas and thus protect the life of Christ in its meaning to us.

Excesses

The excesses of Herod were obvious and numerous. Extremely jealous, he would, indeed, have killed the Christ child. From what we know about Herod's character, the act of killing the boy babies is absolutely believable.

Herod had already killed his favorite wife and two of his sons and later killed a third son because he was afraid they wanted his throne. This atrocious act prompted the Emperor Augustus to say, with a play on Greek words, that it would be better to be Herod's pig *(hus)* than Herod's son *(hurios)*. Fearing that his own death would cause joy in the land, Herod left the command (understandably not carried out) that at his death the oldest child in each home should be put to death, thus hoping to make the nation weep rather than rejoice.

Christians have always had to be on guard to protect Christmas from excesses. The date itself, December 25, was selected as the Christian counterpart to the pagan Feast of Saturnalia, the birthday of the sun. In AD 354, Bishop Liberius of Rome ordered Christmas observed on that date. Christians honored Christ instead of Saturn as the light of the world.

Pagan traditions such as Christmas trees, mistletoe, and the exchange of presents were adapted into the Christian observance. When the Puritans gained power in England, observing Christmas was against the law because of previous excesses and the idea that it was a heathen holiday or a popish practice. The early Americans were also slow to accept Christmas. Most of the states in the union had accepted Christmas as a legal holiday by the mid-1800s. W. A. Carlton, who was dean and professor of church history at Golden Gate Baptist Theological Seminary, once remarked that the power of Jesus Christ to transform the ugly and sordid into something lovely was demonstrated in the transformation of the season into the Christmas celebration.

What are some of the excesses against which we try to protect the life of Christ by protecting the recognition of his birth?

We should guard against the excess of commercialism. Turning the celebration of the birth of Christ into a purely commercial venture is constant danger.

Secularism is an excess against which we should protect Christ and Christmas. Some would make Christmas a totally secular holiday rather than a holy day. Secular interests and pursuits have often been followed at this time with no regard to the spiritual underpinnings.

Sentimentalism must also be watched. There is a tendency to give way to a cheap, sentimental expression of the birth of

Christ. This ignores the meaning of Christ's coming into our world as far as this coming is concerned with the life of the individual or culture.

Gluttonism is always a possibility during the Christmas season. It is an excess. Some people would imbibe in food and drink—and not necessarily alcoholic drinks, though these are often included—to the point of sinfulness.

But one of the greatest excesses against which we would guard in trying to protect the life of Christ in the celebration of his birth is convenientism. It is easy to sell out to popular concepts and practices without giving much thought to their meaning or to their relationship to the Christian faith. Taking the path of convenience rather than conviction is always the easiest way to travel. But it is also always fraught with danger.

Excuses

In protecting the life of Christ by protecting the meaning of his birth, we would also protect him from excuses.

Call up Herod if you could and ask him why he wanted to kill the Christ child. I am quite sure that he would have any number of excuses. Perhaps his first excuse would center on the matter of national security. After all, the country was ruled by Caesar. Caesar was the real king; Herod was a puppet king. If there were any other king running around, even a baby king, national security might be endangered. Why, Rome might move in to make their rule more firm. The whole nation could all suffer.

National interest could have been another excuse. Since Herod was already on the throne and was comfortable with Rome and Rome was comfortable with him, it was in the best interest of the nation for things to remain as they were. Since Herod was the titular king, he would know the national interests better than anyone else.

National policy would surely be on Herod's list of excuses. There could, by definition, be only one king; he was that king. All others would have to go.

But boiled down, Herod had no excuse. Personal selfishness caused him to carry out his atrocious act.

If nothing else, the remembrance of the birth of Christ helps to deliver us from personal selfishness. At this time, we are forced to come out of our shells of selfishness to practice some benevolence, to show some goodwill, to express some kindness, and to at least become aware of the search for peace.

There is no excuse for selfish living when we come to Christmas. The whole story of the birth of Christ and the subsequent events tells of selflessness. The trip to Egypt shows that. Staying in Judea or going back to Gaililee to Nazareth would have been much easier. But because of interest in Christ, selfish elements were swept aside. Mary and Joseph went to Egypt to protect the Christ and Christmas from excuses.

At Christmas, we think of love and what love can do. At the Christmas season a little girl, who obviously did not have much, looked longingly at a display of dolls in a department store window. She was attracted to a rag doll. She had thrown away her old rag doll because it had become old, dirty, and torn. A young man, who was neither well educated nor wealthy, came along the street. He saw the girl gazing into the window with obvious desire. He went into the store, bought the doll, and gave it to the girl.

When asked about his action, the man said, "Ye've crossed the boundary when you begin to love somebody more'n ye do yourself, even if it ain't nobody better'n a rag doll." That is what love can do. The Christmas story protects us from excuses that center in our selfishness.

Escape

But have you noticed one thing about Herod? He did not escape Jesus after all. In spite of all that Herod did to try to keep his throne, Herod did not escape Christ. Herod died soon thereafter of a horrible, loathsome disease. There is no king Herod now.

Herod would not even have been known to any but the historians had not Christ been born in his province. The Herodians were Idumeans who curried the favor of Rome to receive their positions. Herod was the son of Antipater. Upon the death of

HEROD

Antipater, Herod went to Rome where he was assigned the kingdom of Judea and given the title of the king of the Jews. His rule, though carried out with personal cruelty, was rather progressive. He rebuilt cities, established forts, patronized culture and the arts, and rebuilt the Temple in Jerusalem with even greater splendor than during the time of Solomon. He reigned thirty-four years. The birth of Christ in Judea is what has really earned Herod a place in history.

Herod is dead. Despite his cruel attempts to hold his throne, King Herod is dead. Christ is still king, and his kingdom shall last forever. Of his kingdom, there shall be no end. This is the Christmas promise.

That is one reason we must protect Christ and Christmas. If at no other time during the year people hear of Christ and think of Christ, they are forced to think of Christ at Christmas. Amid all of the commercialism and secularism of our modern observance of Christmas, at least one thing breaks through: once, Christ was born on this earth.

I have some good friends of many years standing who are Jewish. I get a card from them each Christmas. Usually it says, "Merry Christmas." They do not attempt to disguise the Christmas season into a holiday season. Once a year, at least, Christ cannot be escaped.

What we must do, then, is to hear the voice of Christ above all of the other clamor of the season. In George Bernard Shaw's *St. Joan* there is a coronation scene in Rheims Cathedral. Joan tells of hearing the voice calling her to deliver France. But Charles, the weak king, interrupted her by saying, "O, your voices, your voices! Why don't the voices come to me? I am king, not you." To which Joan replied, "They do come to you; but you do not hear them. When the angelus rings, you cross yourself and have done with it; but if you prayed from your heart, and listened to the trilling of the bells in the air after they stop ringing, you would hear the voices as well as I do."[1] It is the voice of the Christ that we must hear above all else every Christmas season.

From the very beginning, people have tried to protect Christmas. A very unlikely person in the crowd around the cradle was King Herod. His contribution to the story of the birth of Christ was negative rather than positive. But by his cruel action, he showed us that the life of the Christ must be protected. The best way to protect Christ and Christmas is to accept the Christ of Christmas as Lord and Savior.

Note

1. George Bernard Shaw, *St. Joan*

3

Innkeeper: Providing for His Birth

Imagine you are driving on a long trip. One day you decide you would like to drive an extra half-hour at the end of the day, or maybe fifty more miles before nightfall. Perhaps you decide to get to the next large town if it killed you, no matter how tired you are. When you get to the town and start hunting for a motel, each one you pass flashes a "No Vacancy" sign at you. At first you are a bit selective; then you start getting panicky. It is getting late, and you are tired. The next town is far away. There is no room for you at the Holiday Inn. At that time, an innkeeper who was never very important to you becomes a very important person.

Because this has happened to us we can identify with Mary and Joseph. They tried to find a resting place when they reached Bethlehem just prior to the birth of Jesus. We know more about the story than the busy innkeeper ever did. We know that the pregnant, Galilean peasant woman asking for a room carried the Son of God, our Savior.

The world is an inhospitable enough place to enter without the problem of not having a place to be born. The very Son of God was struggling to be born, and there was no place for him. This gives a new twist to those words in the preface of John's gospel, "He came unto his own, and his own received him not" (John 1:11).

To me there is no sadder expression in the Christmas story than the phrase, "there was no room for them in the inn" (Luke 2:7). Truly there was a crowd at the cradle.

What do we know about the innkeeper who turned the family of the Christ away from the inn but did provide a place for his birth? Very little. Walter Russell Bowie once remarked that the crowded inn of the story became a parable of the human soul. We have all turned away the Christ. But the innkeeper did provide for the birth of the Savior. What can the action of the unnamed and unknown innkeeper mean?

Shut Out

Could it mean that Jesus was shut out? When the innkeeper found no room for Mary and Joseph, they were offered the stable as a birthing place. Could that mean Jesus was shut out?

This is the traditional interpretation. The innkeeper is pictured as a greasy, somewhat ill-tempered old man who brusquely turned them away. We can conceive of him letting them go to the stable only after Joseph's insistence and frantic pleading.

If this traditional view is true, why was Jesus shut out?

Jesus may have been shut out because of busyness. The innkeeper may have been too busy with other things to bother with Mary and Joseph.

We have an Old Testament parable that speaks to this situation. Ahab, the king of Israel, encountered Ben-hadad, the king of Syria, in a battle. When Ahab could have ended Ben-hadad's life and likely ended a lot of strife between the two nations, Ahab allowed Ben-hadad to return home after he had made some vague promises. A prophet disguised himself and approached the king. The prophet told Ahab a story of being entrusted with the life of a prisoner of war with the provision that his life would be forfeited if the prisoner escaped. But while the prophet "was busy here and there, he was gone" (1 Kings 20:40). The king's reply was that the judgment should be carried out; the prophet had failed in his trust. Then the prophet removed his disguise and told King Ahab that he had passed judgment upon himself, for he had allowed Ben-hadad to escape.

A significant part of the story is the prophet's expression, "And as thy servant was busy here and there, he was gone" (1 Kings 20:40). That could be the story of many of our lives. While we have been busy here and there with things for which we can later give no accounting, those valuable things entrusted to us—ministries to perform, responsibilities to keep, children to rear, witness to give, lives to live—have slipped away from us.

We can get too busy for the important things in life. It has been reported that Thomas Carlyle was often short and impatient with his wife. After her death, he read in her diary repeated entries that indicated something of the pain he had inflicted upon her. As he read page after page, he said sadly, "If only I had known. . . . If only I had known. . . ."

If only the innkeeper had known, he would have never turned away the Son of God. But busy people do not know who or what they are turning away. The opportunities will never be acknowledged. The possibilities will never be understood. Busyness can easily result in Jesus being shut out.

Materialism could cause us to shut Jesus out. Money was to be made in that rush season of the Roman census. Since there was money to be made, the innkeeper could not be too concerned with one simple Galilean carpenter. A dramatic monologue entitled, "Yes, I Remember Bethlehem," by Frederick B. Speakman *(The Salty Tang)* speaks to this materialism. The innkeeper says that his father-in-law who owned the inn was almost cheerful, sacking up quite a piece of coin. The fact that they were making so much money was all Caesar's doing, the Caesar whom they resented so much. So turning away another couple would not be so much. They had turned away others during that time.

Each year around Christmas we hear the plea to put Christ in Christmas. Materialism has a devious way of sneaking into our lives before we have realized it. If materialism could have shut out the Christ on that first Christmas, materialism can keep out Christ in succeeding Christmases. Putting Christ into our lives when materialism tries to shut him out is not just a Christmas concern. When money means more than the Master and we push Christ aside, even temporarily, in order to satisfy the material desires of life, we have effectively shut Jesus out by materialism.

Jesus can also be shut out by our priorities. Other guests had arrived at the inn first. They had a place already. If the innkeeper had let Mary and Joseph have a place, then others would have to leave.

This is a very real contemporary problem: when Christ comes into a life, some other things simply must go out of that life. Jesus can share no life with self-centeredness, meanness, littleness, avariciousness, or sensuality.

Most people really do not want to be irreligious or unspiritual. It is just that so many other things occupy the mind that there is little room left for Christ. The priorities of life have not been properly decided. Other matters have gotten there first and have received the attention. Jesus is not given priority.

This leads to the observation that selfishness may have shut Jesus out. All the innkeeper considered was himself and what the census was doing for his business. He was already banking the money. Maybe he was even beginning to think about expansion. Business was good. His interests were being served. That was all that really concerned him at the time.

An ambitious farmer who was unhappy with the yield of his crops heard about a highly recommended new seed corn. He bought some and produced a crop that was so abundant that his astonished neighbors came to see it. They asked him to sell them some of the new seed. But the farmer was afraid that he would lose a profitable competitive advantage. He refused to sell the seed to his neighbors.

The second year the new seed did not produce quite so good a crop. When the third year crop was even worse, the farmer realized that his prize corn was being pollinated by the inferior grade of corn from his neighbor's fields. His selfishness in not sharing the seed corn with his neighbors was making his own crop inferior.

Selfishness never enriches and expands a life. The selfish individual is left to shrink into himself and to find his interests becoming narrower and narrower.

Usually we have been rather harsh in our treatment of the innkeeper. He had shut Jesus out. But could there be more to the story than that?

Helped Out

Could it be that the innkeeper helped out? It could well be that by providing a place in the stable for Jesus to be born, the innkeeper helped out Jesus at a very important time, the time of his birth. William E. Hull, pastor of the First Baptist Church, Shreveport, Louisiana, in a sermon entitled "In Defense of an Innkeeper," has suggested that this incident teaches us the central lesson of the Christmas season, the lesson of lowly service.

Hull also suggested that we may have been laboring under three popular misconceptions in the traditional interpretation of the innkeeper. The first of these misconceptions is the assumption that Mary and Joseph arrived at Bethlehem at the last moment before Jesus' birth. Instead, they may have been there for some time and lived at the inn all that time. Related to this is the conception that we attach to the inn based upon our experience of modern apartment houses or motels. In the crowded, non-private inns of the first century, a degree of privacy and a place where Jesus could be born undisturbed would have been hard to come by. If, indeed, the passage in Luke's Gospel is intended to state that no suitable place for the birth of a child was available to them, rather than that no room at all was available to them in the inn, the role of the innkeeper is different. He may have sent Mary and Joseph to that stable in a cave to provide a place for the birth of the baby. In that case, he did help out Jesus at the time of his birth. He did act in lowly, humble service.

Consider the innkeeper's action in light of the coming of Christ himself. Doubtlessly, the innkeeper would have behaved differently had he known who was being born. He would have been flattered by the idea of welcoming greatness. But Jesus came lowly, meek, and rejected. His symbol was a cross. Only the most sensitive can give meaningful service simply for service's sake.

We focus on our limitations too much. Consider instead the opportunities service of any kind affords us. The innkeeper could have focused only on his limitations—there was no room for Mary and Joseph in the inn. Instead, he looked at the opportunity—there was a stable which could be turned into the birthplace of a child who turned out to be the King of kings. As we consider the opportunities for service, there is nothing that we cannot do.

Whenever I think of a Jewish innkeeper, I think of Mr. Hartmann of the Hartmann Hotel in Tiberias, Israel. This hotel is neither one of the largest nor one of the swankest of the fine hotels in Tiberius on the shore of the Sea of Galilee. The Hartmann Hotel is neat, clean, and accommodating. Mr. Hartmann had various flags flying outside the hotel. A guest observed that no American flag was displayed. And Mr. Hartmann answered that he wanted an American flag, the biggest American flag made. When told that he could not fly the biggest American flag made, he protested by saying, "No. No. 'Cannot' is not a word we use here." And when the progress, development, and growth of Israel is observed, one can believe that *cannot* is not a word that is used there.

Neither should *cannot* be used in Christian service. There is no ministry that cannot be performed for the benefit of someone if we will but do it. The possibilities of Christian ministry and service are limited only by our imaginations and willingness to serve. There is nothing for Christ that cannot be done. By his lowly, courteous service to a couple that had nothing to commend them, the innkeeper always reminds us of this.

When we act in lowly, humble service, we emulate most closely our Savior. Never one to call attention to himself or to advertise his exploits, Jesus gave service quietly, efficiently, and effectively to those persons whom he met. Many of them did not even leave their names upon the record. Most of them had nothing to demand that Jesus should respond to their need and help them. But help them he did. We are most like Jesus when we respond to human needs by helping those who do not have particular claims to make upon us.

In *The Eternal Legacy,* Leonard Griffith tells about a delegate from India who arrived at Evanston, Indiana, for a world-wide meeting of Christians. The delegate had no less than eleven pieces of luggage. Some laymen from the local churches were doing voluntary taxi service that day. This delegate, who was of high birth, stood by while a white-haired gentleman carried all his luggage to the car. It turned out that the chauffeur was none other than the generous benefactor who had given the two mil-

INNKEEPER

lion dollars with which to build McGaw auditorium in which the convocation was being held!

No vacancy. How tragic it is when there is no room for Jesus in a human heart. Do not shut Jesus out. Help him out. Live your life in lowly service as he did.

4
Shepherds: Preserving His Presence

The day after Christmas we live with the ghost of Christmas past.

It doesn't take long for Christmas to pass, does it? There is always an air of expectancy as we await the day of the celebration of the coming of Christ into our world. We have prepared a celebration for his coming; we have done what we can to protect his life in the midst of our busy and hectic schedules. But there must be some way to preserve his presence. With the birth of Christ into our world, the world has changed. But how can we preserve his presence?

Every year the day after Christmas we become very much aware that Christmas is past. The tree so gaily and happily decorated has to be taken down and thrown away. The gifts so beautiful and enticing have been reduced to piles of torn and crumpled wrapping paper. The Christmas dinner that was so delicious has been reduced to dirty dishes and turkey hash. The stores with shelves laden with nice things tastefully arranged look about like the wreck of the Hesperus. And the smiling, accommodating clerks have taken on the look of hasseled, harassed people because of returns and exchanges. You don't hear the Christmas bells and Christmas carols any more; you are back to car horns and rock music.

Can't we preserve Christmas and the presence of Christ in our world? Isn't there some way that we could catch and bottle some of the Christmas spirit? Couldn't we frame some of the moments of ecstasy spent in contemplation of the birth of the Christ child? Shouldn't we solidify some of the attitudes, expansiveness, and feelings we display around Christmas?

SHEPHERDS

The problem of preserving Christmas is not new. Look at two verses in the Christmas story, Luke 2:19-20: "But Mary kept all these things, and pondered them in her heart. And the shepherds returned, glorifying and praising God for all the things that they had heard and seen, as it was told unto them."

Mary kept all those things that had happened, pondering them in her heart. Treasured in her heart were all the events of the first Christmas. She didn't understand all of them. And the whole mystery was not unravelled until the death and resurrection of her firstborn Son who was God's Son. But she preserved them. She preserved his presence by remembering, thinking, and treasuring the events of Christ's coming into the world.

The shepherds sought to preserve Christmas. The shepherds returned to their fields, glorifying and praising God. Their simple, humdrum life had suddenly been transformed by glory. They would not forget that easily or soon. Humble, hard-working people just going about their business of tending sheep had been transformed into witnesses of the wonderful. Their immediate reaction was to praise and glorify God as they returned to their jobs. Their long-term reaction would be to tell and retell their personal stories of these events around campfires for years to come. As they were left alone with their sheep and their thoughts, don't you know they thought about that night many times over?

With the shepherds in the background, we can begin to understand ways we can preserve the coming of Christ into our world and into our lives. From out of the crowd at the cradle, the shepherds come to gaze upon the Christ child. We don't know how many shepherds came. Their presence as a part of the crowd at the cradle was significant. Their attempt at preserving the presence of Christ in their lives helps us know how to do the same thing.

Source

We can preserve Christ's presence by remembering that the source of happiness is God. These shepherds had a happiness they had never experienced before. It had come from God! As the shepherds returned to their fields and their sheep, they praised and glorified God.

Christmas is at the same time the most spiritual and the most secular time of the year. It is spiritual because it focuses on Christ; it is secular because people have bought the lie that happiness rests in things. But it does not. Happiness has its source in God.

Francesco Bernardone was the son of a wealthy merchant in Assisi, Italy. Carefree, lighthearted, he enjoyed the parties and festivities of his upper class set. During a war between Assisi and Perugia, he was freed from imprisonment. He returned home to rounds of parties, but they meant less to him. Embarking on the road to knighthood by fighting with a knight during another war, he soon returned home due to illness. He thought more and more about his meaningless life while he was recuperating. He also thought about the poor people he saw around him. Once a beggar came into the shop and asked him for something in the name of God. After he had chased the man away, Francis realized that he would have given him something if he had asked in the name of the baron. He ran down the street after the man.

While praying in a decaying old chapel one day in 1206, Francis felt that Christ spoke directly to his heart. He felt that Christ told him that he had accepted him. Then Christ said he wanted Francis's labor, his life, his whole being.

Francis told his father that he was selling all his belongings to be an apostle to the poor. His father was angry. His father disinherited Francis in a public ceremony. Francis left Assisi clad in an old mantle lent to him by a gardener. For the next years, Francis stayed alive by begging and by sleeping in the open.

In 1209, Francis came to believe that the words of Jesus in Matthew 10:8-10 were a direct commission to him: "Heal the sick, cleanse the lepers, raise the dead, cast out devils: freely ye have received, freely give. Provide neither gold, nor silver, nor brass in your purses; nor scrip for your journey, neither two coats, neither shoes, nor yet staves: for the workman is worthy of his meat."

Gathering a group of followers, Francis sought to live out that commission. The brothers went in groups of two, singing, preaching, distributing food and clothing to the needy in the city squares, marketplaces, and the countryside.

We know this man as Francis of Assisi and his followers as the Franciscans. They found happiness in following God. They brought spiritual depth and a pattern of unselfish living to a very selfish and secular age. God was the source of happiness for them.

When the shepherds returned, the skies were blank and the road under their feet was only common earth. But they glorified and praised God for what they had seen and heard. Life would never be the same again.

Scene

Where did the shepherds find their happiness? It was found in something very common and simple. It was found in something right where they were. Christ is preserved by remembering that the scene of highest happiness is here.

People have often thought God was very distant. He is not in the clouds of Sinai, behind the curtain of the Temple, or enshrined in a building. God is always right where we are. For the shepherds, God was where they were. God was in a little human child.

A European king worried his court by often disappearing and walking among his people incognito. When he was asked not to do that for security's sake, he would reply that he could not rule his people unless he knew how they lived.

God knows how we live. He knows how we live because he has been one of us and has lived here among us.

We sometimes must be reminded that the scene of God's activity is at the scene of our activity. God's creative activity was performed in the world. God's redemptive activity was also carried out on the earth. This is exactly where we live. We live on this earth. We labor in this world. It does not take some exotic, esoteric place for God's work to be done. God's work can be done where it has always been done: right here on this earth where we live and work.

God cannot be found in some distant day and place if he cannot be found in the here and now. He is served by the simple things we do here.

Ernest Gordon, dean of the chapel at Princeton University, tells that after the Christmas Eve service on the campus one year a rather shabbily dressed man made his way through the crowd of worshipers and thrust a small paper sack in his hand. In the sack were a book of poems and two or three other possessions of such a nature that it was obvious they were the man's most cherished possessions.

But it was Christmas Eve. Students were shouting greetings to the chaplain. He was trying to return their greetings. In the press of the people and general excitement of the happy night the man who had brought the bag of gifts vanished, unidentified.

Two weeks later Gordon picked up the morning paper and saw the man's picture on an inside page. He had been struck and killed while walking along a highway. The encounter had been brief at best. The time for meeting, communication, sharing strength and help was neither offered nor taken. Any opportunity of helping that man was gone forever.

The scene of our work for God is right where we are; and the only time that it can be done is the present. We often may be as surprised as the shepherds to realize that God can break into the normal existence of our lives to transform them into something special and memorable. Where we are is always the scene of God's greatest work—that we should never forget.

Significance

The presence of Christ is preserved by remembering that the significance is unlimited. The shepherds could not have known the full significance of Jesus. But they did know that it was something that went beyond Bethlehem. They did know that his significance was something that went beyond that day.

He would be a king. Likely, none of those shepherds had ever seen a king before, much less been in the presence of a king. But that day, as they gathered around the baby, they were in the presence of a king. This one so humbly born in that cave stable was a king. He was King of kings and Lord of lords. He really rules in human lives. What an unlimited significance that was! It

SHEPHERDS

went far beyond the simple fact of the birth of a baby.

He would be a Savior. Not only was this newborn Child King but he was also Savior. His birth announcement made this clear. In the city of David, Bethlehem, was born one who was born the Savior. He was the Lord Christ. By his coming into the world, he demonstrated the love of God for humankind. By his death on the cross, he demonstrated the length that love would go—it would go even to the length of self-sacrifice of the very Son of God. By his resurrection from the dead, he demonstrated the power of God. God's power goes beyond even the power of death and the grave. As God resurrected Christ to life, he also has the power to give new life to those who trust in him.

We don't really know how God will transform the lives of those who linger in his presence. Without a doubt, the lives of those shepherds were never the same again. In whatever manner God chooses to transform a life, he gives meaning to it. His presence means change.

Bruce Larson, in *The Edge of Adventure,* told of a men's group that was meeting one evening in an office in New York. A man came in whom no one knew. Each thought that he had been referred by someone else in the circle. They suggested he pull up a chair and join the six or eight men who were meeting for fellowship and prayer. The man sat and listened as several of the men talked about their present struggles toward becoming whole people and effective Christians.

Finally the leader turned to the stranger and asked who he was. He replied by saying that his name was Paul and that as long as they were being honest he would be honest too. He was a dope addict. He had come there to rob the office to get a fix, but he thought he had found something better. Paul stayed to pray and asked God for help with his serious problem. He had come into the presence of Christ in the context of the very mundane setting of an office. But while there he had discovered that God was the source of any happiness he could have. The significance of that time spread out into eternity for him.

Christ has come into our world. The world will never be the same again because of that. We would like to preserve his presence. Each year, when the time comes around again to observe and celebrate his birth, we would like to find some special way to preserve his presence. But then we look at the shepherds. Common folk going about their normal affairs doing their regular business, they were ushered into the presence of Christ. From their experience as a part of the crowd at the cradle when the Savior was born, we can see how we, too, can preserve his presence.

Part II
The Crowd in the Country

Even in the country areas Jesus kept running into crowds of people. Wherever he went, he could not escape them. These are people whose names we do not know, but Christ knew them.

5

The Gadarene Demoniac: When Evil Is Destroyed

"And here he met his Waterloo." We have heard that expression a thousand times or more. It has a historical grounding. In 1813, Napoleon was defeated at the Battle of Leipzig. This looked like the end of his military empire. But he hung on. Then in 1814, the troops of the allied nations entered France, and Napoleon was forced to abdicate his throne. He was given sovereignty over the little island of Elba. However, in February of 1815, Napoleon eluded the English fleet and landed again in France. He marched to Paris and was given a tumultous welcome. There he raised another army and laid plans to invade England. He got as far as the little Belgian town of Waterloo. There he was met with forces, mainly English, under the command of Wellington and was decisively beaten. He was then carried by the English fleet to the little island of Saint Helena where his life ended six years later. Napoleon's return to power had lasted one hundred days, then he was decisively and finally beaten. He was so thoroughly beaten that there was no hope of his rising to power again.

The picture of Jesus that we see in Mark 5 shows evil meeting its Waterloo. In coping with Jesus and the power and authority he showed, evil had no hope for victory. Evil was decisively and finally beaten in the life of this helpless and hopeless man—the Gadarene demoniac.

Mark 4—5 tell of an event-filled day. The people had crowded around to hear Jesus teach. He had gone to the shore of the Sea of Galilee and entered a boat which then was cast off a little way from shore. There Jesus taught the people. He taught in parables all day long. Then he and his disciples began to cross to the

THE GADARENE DEMONIAC

other side of the lake, a distance of about eight miles. A storm blew up quickly. Jesus stilled the storm, demonstrating his power over nature. Then they landed on the other side.

The boat landed at a wild and rugged spot. The shore was marked with limestone caves. Many of these caves were used as burial places. The place was grim and ghastly enough during the day, but they landed at evening.

They were met by a madman—a demoniac he was called. He lived among the tombs. He was so uncontrollable that he could not be bound by chains or fetters. He screamed in terror both day and night. He could not be kept clothed. He cut himself with rocks and stones. Surely, no picture could be painted that portrays, in such stark and frank terms, the hold of evil in the life of this man. He was almost inhuman. Yet, when he saw Jesus approaching, the man ran to him, fell before him, and cried, "What do you want with me, Jesus, son of the Most High God? In God's name do not torment me" (Mark 5:7, NEB). It seems uncanny that the unclean spirits always were able to recognize Jesus. Jesus was able to cleanse the man of his demon possession. The demons asked that they not be sent into the wilderness. So Jesus sent the demons into a herd of pigs, who ran headlong over the cliff and were killed.

Evil is shown in its harsh and ugly form. Yet Jesus was able to defeat it. He has this same power today. When we look at the activity of Jesus, we can see the dynamic defeat of evil.

While attempting to escape from the crowds he had seen all day, Jesus met a man whose life was crowded by the forces of evil. But Jesus acted decisively and powerfully with that crowd too.

Demonstration

The decisive defeat of evil demonstrates dynamically the power of God. In this event, we can clearly see the power of Christ over the forces of evil.

The force of evil was so strong in the demoniac's life that it took Jesus awhile to rid the man of his weakness. First, Jesus said authoritatively to the demons, "Come out of the man, thou unclean spirit" (v. 8). This was his usual method. Then he asked the man his name. It was thought that if one knew the name of a demon he would have control over him. In the Bible names stand for nature. So he was asking the man to confess the nature of the powers of evil by which he was enslaved. He answered, "My name is Legion: for we are many" (v. 9). A legion was a Roman force of six thousand men. The man was suggesting that he felt as though he were filled with six thousand demons, well disciplined and strong, each of them able to wreck a man, irresistible in power. Inside of him was a veritable army, plotting his destruction.

William Barclay suggested that this man may have been driven to his state of insanity by the Roman legions. They could be cruel and heartless. Perhaps a legion had come into his town and killed, destroyed, robbed and maimed. The results had driven this man to distraction. Whatever the cause, this man identified the power of evil as legion. At the request of the demons themselves, Jesus sent them into the herd of swine, then to destruction. This was an unanswerable demonstration that the demons had gone out of the man. The unanswerable, dynamic destruction of evil demonstrates the power of God over evil.

Once a little boy's arm was severed by a train. The doctors were able to replace the arm, and it lived. We say that was an unanswerable demonstration of the power of medical science.

Americans orbited the earth in a space capsule and walked on the moon. We say that was an unanswerable demonstration of the power of modern knowledge.

But in the realm of evil, there is no demonstration that is as unanswerable as the power of God in dealing with the hearts of men. The demonic was completely beyond human help. Other people had tried to help him. He had been bound with chains and with fetters. He had been put into isolation from human beings. That was the way demon-possessed people were treated in an effort to cure or at least control them. But this man was completely beyond the aid of humanity. Then Christ came in his power to defeat the evil decisively and completely. We surely say

THE GADARENE DEMONIAC

this is an unanswerable demonstration of the power of God over evil in the human life.

In a sermon, Norman Vincent Peale told of a man who was diagnosed to have a malignant condition which competent specialists had pronounced inoperable and fatal. When asked for the true prospects, the doctor informed the man that he might live six months or maybe only sixty days.

The man went home, knelt down to pray, and admitted to God what a noaccount rotter he had been. He had left his wife to marry his secretary. He was dishonest and profane. He was a heavy drinker. He was a terrible gambler. Having been brought up by Christian parents, he wanted to get right with God before he died. He asked God to take every sin out of him.

God did forgive him. He took the uncleanness out of the man's heart and even removed the lust for gambling.

While reading the Bible, the man came to the words about the wonderful things that would happen if one had faith as a grain of mustard seed. He got the feeling that if he would give himself to God completely God would heal him. He was able to produce "before" and "after" letters from his doctors that a very unusual healing had taken place. Peale verified the experience from others who had known the man well.

But don't look at this thing just in the third person. Don't say, "Well, this happened to the demoniac, and this happened to the man Peale told about. But it can't happen to me." That is a false assumption. If we believe at all in the continuing presence and power of Christ through the Holy Spirit, such experiences can happen.

The Lord can defeat the hate in our hearts.

The Lord can defeat the pettiness of character.

The Lord can defeat the malicious, hurtful spirit that we sometimes show.

The Lord can defeat the urge to gossip and malign.

The Lord can remove the lust from our heart.

The Lord can remove the temptation to lie, to cheat, to deal falsely, to steal.

In short, God is still in the business of defeating evil. It may not be in such spectacular terms as sending demons into pigs and pigs over cliffs, but it is just as real and just as meaningful and just as helpful to the person benefitting from it.

Disturbance

When the pigs tumbled over the cliff, the swineherds immediately ran into town to tell the people what had happened. Then the swineherds and the townspeople all rushed out to the place. There they found the demented man—the madman, the demoniac—clothed and in his right mind, sitting at the feet of Jesus.

What a transformation! The demoniac had been unclothed, raging, unable to sit still, throwing rocks and insults at any who came by and bashing and cutting himself with the stones. Now he was sitting quietly at the feet of Jesus. Their neighbor was now in his right mind. A man had been restored to usefulness. Wouldn't you think those people would be thrilled? But not on your life.

These people were unhappy. Their business had been disrupted. All they could see were the two thousand dead pigs. What are two thousand pigs in relation to a man restored? But this event had disturbed their business. The presence of Christ was a disturbing factor. So they asked him to leave.

This was the second request made of Jesus. The demons had requested to go into the swine. Now the local people are requesting Jesus leave their shores. He did.

The presence of Jesus is always disturbing. We cannot face Jesus and be unaffected. Whenever we see Jesus and whenever we honestly face him and his demands, we are disturbed. It is absolutely impossible for life to go on as usual.

When Christ comes, our comfort might be disturbed. When we have met Christ and he has worked his transforming grace in our hearts, we cannot possibly be as comfortable as we were before. This is what happened at Gerasa. These people just were not comfortable with Jesus around. His presence was an ever-present reminder that they thought more of pigs than people.

We cannot be comfortable about the plight of other people. Christianity ought to give us a social consciousness.

THE GADARENE DEMONIAC

We cannot be comfortable about the spiritual condition of other people. Christianity ought to give us a concern.

We cannot be comfortable about bad treatment of other people. Christianity ought to give us a compassion.

We cannot be comfortable with our own preconceived notions and ideas and prejudices. Christianity ought to get us thinking and examining.

When Christ comes, he might disburb your possessions. This was the main reason the townspeople wanted Christ to leave. He had begun to disturb their possessions. We see the same thing in the experience of Paul. A young girl who had soothsaying powers was being used by unscrupulous men in Philippi. Paul healed her, and her owners were so incensed that they demanded that Paul and Barnabas be jailed. When Christ truly works in your heart you can no longer be selfish and self-minded. Zacchaeus gave half of his goods to the poor. The rich young ruler, unwilling to part with his possessions, rejected Christ. When Christ comes, he might disturb your possessions. Accepting Christ will mean that you will need to share and to give and to tithe. But all this will not be done in a legalistic spirit but out of a heart of love and gratitude.

When Christ comes, he might disturb your beliefs. If you are real frank with the Holy Spirit, you will probably see that some of your beliefs need disturbing. There are some parts of the gospel message we have not begun to implement in our lives. Elton Trueblood says that we are as shocked to see people practice our faith as we are to hear them deny it. Christ will come to you to show you that belief in him is more than just attending church once a week. To be Christian means to make Christ Lord of life and let him rule in all areas of life: social, business, home, religious.

Sadly, Christ honored the people's request to leave them alone. It is a dangerous thing to request the Spirit of God to leave us alone—he might just do it. Sometimes the worst possible thing for us might be for the Lord to grant us our prayer. The psalmist had something like this in mind when he wrote, "And he gave them their request; but sent leanness into their soul" (106:15). As Peter Marshall said, "Praying is dangerous business. The Lord might just decide to answer your prayer as you prayed it."

Disciple

The now-healed demoniac asked to be allowed to accompany Jesus. This was the third request made of Jesus. The man wanted to be one of Jesus' disciples. Whereas the other two requests made of Jesus were allowed, this one was turned down. But the man was not denied altogether. Jesus told him, "Go home to thy friends, and tell them how great things the Lord hath done for thee, and hath had compassion on thee" (Mark 5:19).

Sometimes the hardest assignment is to witness of the power and love of God to our friends. But it is the most important assignment. These are the people who know you. They know what you were. But they can see what God has done with you. They can, or ought to be able to, judge that surely the power of God is active to change the lives and hearts of sinful men. I am convinced that the most effective evangelistic testimony is the simple statement to another person of what God has done for you. Our duty is not to look for some place where being Christian is easier but to be Christian where we are.

One of Rudyard Kipling's poems is entitled "Mulholland's Contract." Mulholland was a cattleman on a cattleboat. Once on a voyage a violent storm broke out and the cattle broke loose between the decks. Mulholland was in imminent danger of dying beneath their plunging hooves and horns. So Mulholland made a contract with God that if he made it to port alive he would exalt the name of God and praise it until he received further orders. Miraculously he was preserved, and he determined to keep his contract. He spoke to God in prayer about this contract. The answer that he received was that God never put on his ministers more than they could bear, so he was to go back to the cattleboats and preach the gospel there. That had not been Mulholland's idea at all. The last thing he wanted to do was to preach on the cattleboats where everybody knew him. But he was an honest man, and he did it even though it meant that he could not preach the gospel "handsome and out of the wet." It is natural for everyone to want to preach religion handsome and in the dry, but Jesus says to us what he said to the healed demoniac at Gerasa and what he said to Mulholland: "Go back to the people who know you best, and be a Christian there."

What a witness the restored man had! He had recognized the person of Christ. He had experienced Christ's saving and cleansing work. He had made the equation of God and Jesus; he knew himself to be a recipient of the divine mercy.

What a witness this man had! Why, it is exactly the witness that we have. And what the healed man was to do, we are to do. Jesus demanded no more of him than he demands of each of us.

But there is one difference. This man did as Jesus said. The man immediately set to the task Jesus had given him (Mark 5:20). Doesn't that shame us? Can't we immediately see how very lax we have been? The grace of God has invaded our experience and claimed our lives. The very least we can do is to spread this word, to tell others of the saving grace of the Lord Jesus Christ. This is the secret of Christianity. This is the ancient pattern with which Christianity began. For it to be dynamic, and real, and living, and vibrant, we must make it the modern pattern. It is your responsibility. What are you going to do with it?

The dynamic destruction of the power of evil is possible. Christ can enter the life of anyone to destroy the power of evil in that life. But when he does, the presence of Christ is a disturbing matter. But out of this experience with Christ, there came a disciple—one dedicated to telling of Jesus' grace. This is where we fit in. We must do it. While leaving the crowd, Jesus found a crowd: a crowd of demons in one man. Jesus destroyed the power of evil.

6

The Rich, Young Ruler: When Life Is Explained

The good life.

Advertisers have tried to convince us that the good life is found in their products: a housing development or a resort community. Should we go out to see such developments the pitch is made that we can have the good life of privacy, recreation, and fun. Maybe the product is designed for the person who has everything—everything but that product which will make life complete.

The good life is defined by what we *have* and *where* we are. It is rarely defined by *what* we *are*.

The good life may be defined in sensual terms. Girls and goods become the goals that are presented to the individual. In slick paper, multicolored photography and lurid writing, these concepts are pushed. When one has excited the senses sufficiently, he is assumed to have found the good life.

Or the good life may be defined in material terms. When one has gathered around him the right amount of the right kind of things, he has attained the good life. This feeds into what has been called the big lie: Life consists in the things we have.

Jesus once explained the meaning of life to a young man. He was the man who had everything: youth, wealth, prestige, power, and background. But he came to Jesus because he had not found life satisfying. Something was still lacking in his life. He knelt before Jesus and asked: "Good master, what good thing shall I do, that I may have eternal life?" (Matt. 19:16).

We call this man the rich young ruler. His story is told in all synoptic Gospels (Matt. 19:16-22; Mark 10:17-22; Luke 18:18-23). We must read all three accounts to know that the man

THE RICH, YOUNG RULER

was a rich, young ruler. Only Matthew tells us that he was young, and only Luke records that he was a ruler. All three Gospels testify that he was rich.

The man was rich, but his life was not rich. In spite of all of his affluence, physical comforts, prestige and pleasure, he still needed something more. For some reason, he felt Jesus Christ could supply what he needed.

But the rich, young ruler was looking for satisfaction in his activity. What good *thing* could he do, he asked. He felt that there was some good deed that he could perform that would assure for him the eternal life he desired. Jesus' reply indicated that it is not what we *do* but what we *are* that makes the difference in life.

Jesus outlines some of the Commandments. Those are the Commandments dealing with man's relationship to man.

The young ruler replied that he had kept these Commandments all of his life. I once thought that this reply was an arrogant boast. Who could keep the Commandments? But I have become more convinced that it was the honest answer of a pious Jew. As far as he could and as far as he was concerned, he had kept the Commandments.

But if keeping the Commandments had not brought satisfaction to life, what could? This was the heart of his question. He was asking Jesus to explain life to him. He needed a richness, a fullness, a satisfaction, a significance in life. Where could he find that? If not keeping the Law, then perhaps he could find the meaning of life by doing a wonderful deed.

Jesus put his finger on the man's problem. In his answer, Jesus hit an open nerve. If the man wanted the eternal life, he would have to sell all that he had, give it to the poor, and follow Jesus. This answer ran counter to everything the pious Jew had believed. Riches were the evidence of God's favor. If one were rich, he was blessed by God. Nothing else was needed to show God's acceptance of that person. But Jesus made a radical demand for sovereignty in this man's life.

As long as wealth stood in the way, this young man would not put Jesus Christ and the will of God first in his life. As long as he had wealth, he would give it first claim on his time, his energy, his thought, and his devotion.

The key is in the phrase, "Follow me." In following Jesus, life is explained. The life of faith that is eternal, not only eternal in quantity but also eternal in quality, is found in following Jesus in obedience and faith. This is the good life. This the young man was unwilling to do.

As life was explained by Jesus when one came rushing out of the crowd to inquire about it, there are some constant elements that help us to see life's true meaning.

Concept

When Jesus explained life, we get the concept of life being made up of decisions. These decisions may not seem so big or so important at the time they are made. But when we start analyzing our lives, we discover that we are where we are because of the many decisions that we have made from time to time. We may stand at the threshold of watershed decisions and never realize it.

This rich, young ruler was faced with life's greatest decision. It would determine the course of his life. But he did not realize it. He blew it. He was on a threshold and never was aware of it. And so it is with us many times. The great decisions, the big things, are not the ones that throw us most often. The day-to-day decisions that we must make result in the charting of our courses.

The young man could not make the decision of self-negating love that would put him before Jesus and the world with just faith. All of his life he had held onto other things—his wealth, specifically—in order to have meaning and security. Now Jesus was asking him to face the world in bare faith. That he could not do.

Each decision, each experience becomes a preparation for what we must ultimately do when we make the life-changing decisions. In 1754, George Washington, in his early twenties, was defeated at Fort Necessity. He was accused of taking hasty action to get glory for himself before reinforcements came. A report on French plans was denounced as a crooked scheme to advance the interests of a private land company. His officers were called drunken debauchers. But Douglas Southall Freeman, Washington's biographer, observed that when one is about to exclaim about some mistreatment that it is an outrage, he reflects and says instead that it is a preparation.

So Jesus explained life in these terms. Even inquiring of Jesus about the way to eternal life, the rich young ruler was not prepared for the big decision because he had always deferred the little decisions. Life was formed. His decision was already made because he had made it a little at a time whenever the question of trust was advanced. He had great possessions. In the end, he trusted the possessions more than he trusted Christ.

Challenge

A challenge was inherent in the reply Jesus made to this young man. It was the challenge to live with Christ and to really find the good life. In explaining life, Jesus Christ explained it as a challenge.

The challenge was, How much do you really want Christianity? Robert Louis Stevenson, in one of his novels, spoke about the "malady of not wanting enough." This malady has all but become an epidemic. Amid all of the things that we want and the industry that is committed to whetting our appetites for more, we suffer from the malady of not wanting enough. We want the good life, but we are unwilling to be disciplined. We want goodness, but we are unwilling to pay the price by saying no on occasion. We want success, but we are not willing to struggle and to sacrifice. The rich young ruler wanted eternal life, but he did not want it enough. Perhaps he thought that the good thing he could do to inherit eternal life would consist in giving to another charity or heading another committee.

The Russian author Dostoevski wrote a story about a woman who died and was told that she would be taken to heaven if she could remember one unselfish act she had performed while on earth. She could remember only one. She had once given a beggar a withered carrot. Down the limitless space that separates heaven from hell, the carrot was lowered on a slender string. Desperately the woman grasped it and slowly began to rise. Suddenly she felt a weight holding her back. Looking down, she saw other tormented souls clinging to her and hoping to rise with her. She cried to them to let go; that was her carrot. At that point, the string broke. She fell down into the pains of hell still clutching her carrot.

Our challenge is to live unselfishly in this world, to serve God by serving others. While the rich, young ruler may not have committed adultery or stolen or defrauded others or coveted their goods, the evidence does not seem to indicate that he lived unselfishly. He did not seem willing to give from what he had to alleviate human need. When Jesus asked him to spend his possessions and himself on others, he could not do it. He could not rise to that challenge.

We have the challenge to go out into this hungry, divided, confused world and apply some principles of love, mercy, justice, faith, and dedication. The world can be remade as we accept the challenge before us in the Spirit and power of Christ.

We have a challenge to carry the witness of Christ into the world. Bill Glass, former all-pro football player and now evangelist, said,

I have found a fulfillment in pro football. Somehow, I feel at home there. I'm afraid that it's too often true that we count the fulfillment of our mission in life as a matter of having attained some measure of perfection in a job of one kind or another. There is no doubt that God does want you to be successful as a teacher, mechanic, housewife, or in whatever vocation you choose. But that is not all of it; as a matter of fact, that isn't even the most important thing. Our job as Christians is first and foremost to penetrate the world with a Christian witness.[1]

We have a challenge to examine all that makes up our lives. In our preoccupation with things and events, in our busyness with all that crowds our schedules, in our interest in the many things that clamor for our attention, we may simply crowd Christ out of our lives. With the rich, young ruler, we are challenged to

THE RICH, YOUNG RULER

look at how our lives are organized and what has become the integrating center for life.

H. M. Weathersby was for many years the dean of Louisiana College in Pineville, Louisiana. When he spoke in chapel, we could almost be sure that he would read Psalm 1. Also, the chances were pretty good that he would tell the story of the country boy who went to the circus. This boy had saved his money all year in anticipation of going to the circus. Finally the circus came to town. Hardly able to contain himself, he rode his mule to town, tied it up, and ran to see the circus. He watched the parade, then followed the crowd out to the circus grounds. He saw a tent and went in to see the sideshow. He asked a man where to pay his money; the man readily agreed to take it. When the boy came out of the sideshow, he saw a crowd coming out of the big top. He asked them where they had been and they replied that they had been to the circus. He had spent his money, used his time, wasted his opportunity, and had never got around to seeing the circus. The main attraction had been crowded out of his life.

The rich, young ruler did not respond to his challenge. We must be sure that we do.

Commitment

As Jesus explained life, our commitments will be involved. The whole matter, as far as this rich, young ruler was concerned, turned on the matter of commitment. He was not willing to commit himself to Christ in order to reach the aspiration that he had.

The same is true for each of us. Whatever we are will depend on the commitment that we make to Christ as Lord, Savior, Leader of life.

In this commitment there is a distinction between being respectable and being good. This young man was respectable without being positively good. And so can we.

We are often willing to fall back on our negative goodness, the things that we have done that make us respectable in society, without reaching out to a positive goodness. The rich, young ruler refused to take the steps that would eventuate in positive goodness and grace expressed toward others.

Leonard Griffith, in *Encounters with Christ,* observed that in Dante's hell not a single sinner in the "Circle of the Avaricious" can be identified. All of them are nameless and faceless. The man who values possessions above personality finds his nemesis in the ultimate loss of his own personality. For a few acres of land and a few bags of gold, he surrenders everything that could make him a person, a child of God throughout eternity.

There is a standard in this commitment. The standard is the faith in Jesus Christ that commits all of life to him. Jesus would not lower his standard to make an easy convert.

The key to the experience is not the command to the young man to sell what he had and to give that to the poor. Other rich persons, Nicodemus and Joseph of Arimethea, for instance, were not given that command. The key to the whole passage is not "go, sell" but "come, follow me."

Jesus made that clear in the discussion with the disciples that followed the young man's leaving. The disciples could not understand what had happened. They could not understand why this man was not already marked for the kingdom of God. Evidently God had favored him. Jesus said to them, "How hard it will be for those who have riches to enter the kingdom of God!" (Mark 10:23, RSV). Upon seeing their amazement, Jesus expanded it to say, "Children, how hard it is for them that *trust* in riches to enter into the kingdom of God!" (Mark 10:24, author's italics).

That is the answer: It is impossible to trust in anything except Jesus Christ as personal Savior and enter into the kingdom of God. Jesus used an expression of evident exaggeration: It is easier for a camel to go through a needle's eye than for a person with riches to enter the kingdom of God. Why? Not because of the riches. People with riches and generous spirits have done much for the kingdom of God. The problem is that a rich man has a tendency to trust in his riches. Riches can do a lot of things. People who are rich are prone to trust in riches. Riches can do a lot of things, but they cannot bring salvation. Trust and

THE RICH, YOUNG RULER

faith in Jesus Christ alone can do that.

These perilous times call for commitment. In 1860, Robert E. Lee was in Texas when that state overrode the objections of Sam Houston and sided with South Carolina and Alabama to join the Confederacy. Colonel Lee was told to surrender United States property. He promptly replied by saying that he was an officer of the United States and a Virginian. He would not take orders from Texans! A few months later, Lee identified himself with the Confederacy and against the United States. It was a part of his code of honor to protect family and state. He had made a commitment.

Life needs to be explained for us. Life holds many riddles. How may we come to eternal life? Jesus explains life to us while he explained it to the rich young ruler, who came to him from out of the crowd. In the end, the life that is fit for eternity and that expresses eternal values in the living of it is that life that trusts in Christ. Life is found and explained in Christ.

Note

1. Bill Glass, *My Greatest Challenge*, p. 180. Used by permission of Word Books, Publisher, Waco, Texas 76703.

7

The Paralytic: When Ministry Is Performed

Frank Boreham of Australia had a friend whom everyone in town called Uncle Jed. He had won quite a reputation in the community as Mr. Fixit. If anything went wrong, they called Uncle Jed. He could fix it. One day Uncle Jed was putting a new hinge on an old gate; Boreham was watching with admiration.

Boreham mentioned that Uncle Jed was always fixing something. Uncle Jed replied by saying there were only four sorts of things in the world, only one of them was his business, and he would like to do that well. Pressed for an explanation, he described the four sorts of things in the world as he saw them.

First were the things that never needed repair; he did not need to worry over them. Then there were the things that could not be fixed; he saw no need to fret over them. Some things will repair themselves if given a fair chance; Uncle Jed saw no need to go meddling with them. But there were also the things that would go from bad to worse unless someone repaired them; that was his business, and he liked to do it well.

That also is ministry: to attempt to bring help and healing where it is needed. It occurs because someone cares. The ethic of the serving church and the caring Christian is written deeply and indelibly into the Christian life.

The caring concern that issues in ministry to others started with Jesus Christ. Throughout his ministry, he would reach out into the crowd to touch the life of an individual in order to minister to his need and to give him hope.

One time Jesus was in Capernaum (Mark 2:1). Through teaching, answering questions, and healing by God's power, Jesus had attracted such a crowd of people that no one else could enter the house. Then some enterprising men brought a paralyzed

THE PARALYTIC

friend to Jesus. Undeterred by the fact that they could not enter the house, the determined friends climbed to the flat roof of the house, tore a hole through the roofing, and lowered the man on his pallet right before the Master. The synoptic Gospels tell the story (Mark 2:2-12; Matt. 9:1-8; and Luke 5:17-26).

In the very midst of a crowd, ministry was performed. Jesus responded to the faith of the friends and healed the man. But he also gave the man more than he asked for: Jesus forgave the man's sins. In this experience, we can see some of the things that happen when persons care enough to minister.

Purpose

The purpose of ministry is to bring people to Christ.

These friends, assumed to be four so that each could hold a rope at one end of the pallet, were determined to bring their friend to Jesus. Ministry always has the underlying purpose of bringing people to Jesus.

Ministry might be expressed in such diverse ways as a wellbaby clinic, a senior citizen's activity, or a literacy program. But the ultimate intention is that, through the care of others, people might be brought into the presence of Jesus.

When Jesus saw the faith of the friends who had brought the man to him, he told the man his sins were forgiven. Bringing people into the presence of Jesus results in the forgiveness of sin and new life.

When we have brought a person into the presence of Jesus through a caring ministry, we have done all that we can do. We cannot force forgiveness on him. We cannot make him believe. We cannot coerce him into the kingdom of God. At that time, the grace of God moves into his life to remake him as God intended. The friends could bring the man to Jesus; they could not heal him. Only Jesus could do that.

A man described his conversion at an Alcoholic Anonymous meeting. He said that he once had a very intricate watch. When something went wrong with it, he knew he could not fix it. He knew that his best hope was to take it to the man who knew the inner workings of a watch. It dawned on him one day that his life was like that watch: intricate, yet wrong in the works. He had tried to fix it himself but could not. He realized that his best hope was to go humbly to his Maker and ask him to straighten him out. And he did.

Possibilities

Where are the possibilities for ministry? They are everywhere. Many people would have looked at the crowd around Christ and despaired. They would have seen the crowded house and come to the conclusion that there was no possibility for ministry there.

But the possibilities for ministry abound. They are limited only by our imagination and ingenuity.

In *Beggars in Velvet,* Carlyle Marney told about a man who came to see him about every three years. This man with soft blue eyes, a very kind voice, and a mild manner wrote like Sören Kierkegaard, according to Marney. Once this man had expected to be a minister in a Christian church, but he simply did not fit. Elements of freedom and inspiration in his personality just could not be confined to the institutional church. On one visit, Marney asked the man what he did to exercise his calling since he had no congregation and no pulpit. The man answered by asking, "Who said I have no congregation?" He then said that there is a lot of grief and pain he could sit beside.

None of us would have to look far to find a lot of grief and pain we could sit beside. All around us are people who hurt: the disenfranchised, the lonely, the hungering, the wounded, the sorrowing, those who are alone in the world.

We have no way of knowing whether the friends in the Gospel accounts were relatives or neighbors. But we do know that they were people who saw the possibility of ministry because they had sat beside some grief and pain.

Performance

As we look at this encounter of Christ with the paralytic man in the crowd, we can see something about the performance of ministry.

Priority is the first matter in the performance of ministry.

THE PARALYTIC

These persons had ministry as a priority. If ministry had not been a priority for them, they would have become discouraged and left. But because ministry was a priority to them, the man was brought to Jesus and healed. Ministry is never done automatically or accidentally. It is done because someone thought it was important enough to act.

Patience is also an element in the performance of ministry. Had these friends not been patient persons, ministry would never have been performed. The man would never have been either healed or forgiven. Most of us act out what one bumper sticker reads, "Lord, give me patience and give it to me now!" We do not really want to wait for something to develop. We want it instantly.

These friends who cared patiently figured out a plan and carried it out. They removed the roofing material and lowered the man on his pallet into Jesus' presence.

But there really can never be ministry without *persistence*. Persistence paid off. Less persistent people would have returned home.

We think of Augustine, bishop of Hippo, who became a saintly scholar. But he had lived a profligate life as a youth. His mother, Monica, was a Christian who pled with him, preached to him, and prayed for him. He left North Africa to go to Italy, and his mother despaired of his ever finding Christ. A Christian pastor assured her that it was impossible for a child of such tears and prayers to perish. And he did not. In Italy, Augustine found Christ through the preaching and the direction of Ambrose. Persistence brought him to Christ.

Persistence in ministry will pay off with spiritual dividends. With persistence, ways can be found to minister. Perhaps an apartment complex cannot be penetrated. But then someone who lives there becomes a Christian, and the way is opened for a ministry from a new base.

Promise

The promise of ministry is forgiven sin and renewed life.
When Jesus saw the man before him, he said, "Man, your sins

are forgiven you" (Luke 5:20, RSV). But the scribes and the religious leaders, who were crowded in the house, began to get upset. They murmured that no one could forgive sins but God. That was just the point.

Jesus was acting in the power of God to forgive sin. This is the promise of ministry: When people are brought into the presence of Jesus, their sins can be forgiven and their lives can be renewed. Jesus delivered exactly what he promised.

One writer observed that the neighborhood bar is a popular place because it delivers what it promises. It provides the intoxication that it advertises. Jesus promises forgiveness and new life. He can make good on that promise when people are brought into his presence through a caring ministry.

But the spiritual had to be demonstrated through the physical. Jesus knew that the religious leaders were questioning his ability to forgive sin. So he asked them which would be easier to say: one's sins were forgiven or he was healed of a paralysis? Obviously, it would be easier to *say* that sins are forgiven. That is an internal thing and hard to prove. Had he told the man to rise up and walk, he would have had to prove that he had this power. But in order for them to know that Jesus had the power to forgive sins, he commanded the man to rise up and walk. And he did!

In the ancient Jew's understanding of illness, there was a relationship between sin and sickness. By Jesus forgiving the man's sins, there could be no doubt that his life had been renewed. Both physically and spiritually, he had been made right with God.

Jesus was also able to demonstrate his spiritual power by his physical actions. That is the only way some people will ever understand spiritual power. That is also the promise of ministry: Spiritual power can be demonstrated by physical actions.

In his memorable sermon "Handling Life's Second Bests," Harry Emerson Fosdick told of William Duncan who gave himself to the cause of missions. In time, he was sent by his mission board to a little Indian island called Metlakatla off Alaska. Those Indians were a poor, ignorant, miserable tribe. Their morals were vile beyond description.

Dean Brown of Yale University visited Metlakatla after William Duncan had been there for forty years. He reported that every Indian family lived in a separate house with all the decent appointments of home life. They had a bank, a cooperative store, a saw mill, a box factory, and a salmon cannery run by Indians in a profitable industry. There was a school where Indian boys and girls learned to read, write, think, and live. There was a church where an Indian minister preached the gospel of eternal life; an Indian musician, who was once a medicine man playing a tom-tom, played a pipe organ. The congregation of Indians sang the great hymns of the church to the praise of God. This was all possible because a man named William Duncan cared and showed spiritual power through physical actions.

When the people in that crowded house saw what had happened, "Amazement seized them all, and they glorified God and were filled with awe, saying, 'We have seen strange things today' " (Luke 5:26, RSV). Certainly these are strange things. These are things of spiritual power that occur when people minister. When out of the crowd that surrounded the Christ, ministry was performed, a life was totally changed. The strange things can become the commonplace things as ministry is performed.

Some years back C. W. Brister of Southwestern Baptist Theological Seminary wrote a book entitled *People Who Care.* When he mentioned the title to a friend, the friend replied by saying, "You mean there are still some of *those* people around?" There *are* some of those people around. There always will be some of those people around as Christ touches and transforms them from out of the crowd.

8

The Syro-Phoenician Woman: When Faith Is Demonstrated

In an article in *Time* magazine on November 1, 1971, Clare Boothe Luce wrote that a great man is one sentence. History has no time for more than one sentence, and it is always a sentence with an active verb. The sentence she used to describe Dwight D. Eisenhower was: "He led the victorious armies of the alliance in the greatest war in history." For John F. Kennedy, she chose this sentence: "He challenged the might of the Soviet Union in the Western Hemisphere and won—short of war."[1]

If you were to try to summarize your life in one sentence, what would that sentence be? Is there a good, one sentence summary of your life? Is there a sentence with an active verb that would express the impact of your life?

Jesus used one sentence once to characterize a woman. It was a short sentence, of only four words. This woman was not a Jew; she was a Canaanite. We know very little about her. In fact, we do not even know her name. She came from a country north of Palestine, about where Lebanon is today, that was hostile to the Jews. She was presumably married, with at least one child. But that is about all that we know. We do not know whether she was a good or bad woman. We do not even know whether she was a religious woman or an irreligious woman. We do know that she was a troubled and agitated woman whose daughter was possessed by a demon. We only know her in a single encounter with Jesus and his characterization of her: "Great is your faith!" (Matt. 15:28, RSV).

Some people are more qualified to make judgments than others. In September, 1979, Irl Allison died in Austin, Texas. Irl Allison was the founder of the National Guild of Piano Teachers. He also was the founder of the Van Cliburn Interna-

THE SYRO-PHOENICIAN WOMAN 61

tional Piano Competition. If a pianist were to play and I were to remark that it was a great rendition of that piece of music, you could take the remark or leave it. A piano critic I am not. But if Irl Allison had commented that the pianist's rendition of that piece of music was brilliant, then the comment would have been taken seriously. Jesus was qualified to make a judgment on faith. He looked for faith. But he did not always find it. He did not always find faith in his disciples. We do not find a place in the Gospels where he said, "Great is your fiath," to them.

Jesus and his disciples had gone into the area north of Galilee around the Phoenician cities of Tyre and Sidon for a time of rest. Jesus needed to get away from both the press of the crowds and the demands upon him. He needed physical rest. But he also needed a teaching time for the disciples. This would be a time that he could teach them; they could share some quality time together.

But as Jesus attempted to escape the crowds, he ran into this Syro-Phoenician woman who called on him for help. From out of the crowd, while attempting to get away from the crowd, Jesus had a call for help. From this woman came a demonstration of faith.

In these days, the word for our lives needs to be *faith*. That should be the summary of our lives: Great is your faith. The demonstration of faith is seen in this unknown woman, who called to the Christ from out of the crowd in the country.

Realization

One thing that must be said about this woman is that she turned to Jesus for help. We have lives of faith when we realize the Source of help. This realization always brings us right to Jesus. Jesus is our source of help.

Likely Jesus had gone into this area to escape the clamors for help and to have some time alone with the disciples to teach them. But here was a most unusual person calling for help. When she needed help, she turned to Jesus.

To find help from Jesus, we will have to cross barriers. This woman crossed barriers to come to Christ. Despite the barriers of race, sex, religion, and prejudice, she turned to Jesus. Jesus was a Jew. She was a Canaanite, people who did not mix well because they had contempt for one another. Women were not supposed to speak publicly to men, according to the patterns of the time; but she called out publicly and repeatedly to Jesus. Canaanites were not Jews, therefore, their religion was very different. How much she knew about Jesus or about Judaism we have no way of knowing; but she was willing to cross the barrier of religion in order to reach Jesus in her call for help. But she leaped across these barriers to call for Christ.

We always face barriers in our approach to the Christ. Leonard Griffith, in *Gospel Characters,* pointed out that we always have to cross the barriers of time, culture, and pride when faith turns to Jesus for help. Ours is a different time from the time in which Jesus lived. The difference in time helps to explain the difference in culture. Rather than an ancient, Near Eastern culture, we live in a modern, Western culture. They are very far removed from one another. A world that has gained more and more mastery over the natural feels less inclined to look for the supernatural for help. These barriers must always be crossed as we leap back over time, culture, and pride to reach the gentle Nazarene who helps us in our deepest needs.

In ministry, we are "barrier busters." Each time a person is reached in ministry, barriers have to be breached. The psychological barrier that prevents one from admitting that he needs help must be breached. The personal barrier makes it difficult for one to admit his need for help. That the basis of the problem may be spiritual due to sin and alienation from God creates a sin barrier that is difficult to hurdle. Then there is the spiritual barrier of going to Jesus Christ as the Source of help that must be burst. Barriers abound. But as we come to the realization that Jesus is our Source of help, we will be willing to cross those barriers to meet the Christ.

William Peter Blatty's book *The Exorcist* is the story of a sophisticated actress in Washington, D.C., who was separated from her husband. She had a twelve-year-old daughter who was normally a quiet and cheerful child. The child began behaving strangely. From her mouth came revolting obscenities and blasphemies; her features contorted. She spoke with the croaking voice of an old man. She became so violent and so physically ill that she had to be strapped down to the bed. The bed moved up and down of its own accord. Physicians and psychiatrists were baffled. The actress mother nearly went out of her mind. Finally, a Roman Catholic priest was consulted. He concluded that the child was possessed of a demon that had to be exorcised. This went against all reason and contemporary explanations. The woman was not a Christian. She neither understood demon possession nor the Catholic Church's ritual of exorcism. But she was desperate, and her desperation drove her to a representative of Jesus Christ for help. Without going into the matter of demon possession or the rite of exorcism, the point is that when this woman needed help she went to Christ through one of his ministers.

When we see that we need help, we turn to Christ. That is living lives of faith: realizing that the Source of help is Jesus Christ. This should be our first step rather than the desperation last step it so often is. Jesus Christ is our Source of help.

Refusal

We live lives of faith when we refuse to be intimidated by others. This Syro-Phoenician woman refused to be intimidated by others. One of our failures of faith is that we are so easily intimidated. When what we want does not come about immediately, we back off, quit, or admit defeat. Jesus told several parables about perseverance in prayer. We should read the parables again and take them to heart. We can also look to this woman as an example of perseverance.

Some people sought to intimidate this woman in a number of ways. She refused to be intimidated by any of them.

First was the silence of Jesus. She called to Jesus, and he did not answer her. His failure to answer did not make the woman quit calling after him for the help she desired. His initial response to her was silence: "But he did not answer her a word" (Matt. 15:23, RSV).

She continued to call on Jesus in a developing faith. In a faith that developed from calling him "Son of David," which was a title of respect indicating a powerful person, to "Lord," which would indicate his authority even over demons, she continued to call on him. The silence of Jesus did not deter her.

One of the things that bothers us most is the silence of the Savior when we call on him. We want instant answers and immediate results. Do we not also need time for faith to develop and to understand that Jesus answers in his own way and in his own time?

Can You Wait Till Friday? by Ken Olson, tells a story about William Wallner, a Lutheran minister in Prague, Czechoslovakia during World Warr II. Wallner served a congregation that was small at first but grew as refugees fled from Germany. At one time, Wallner was preaching five sermons on Sunday to over twenty-five thousand people in several languages. In his church were over three thousand Jews, including a rabbi who had become a Christian as he fled from Hitler and Germany. One Jew was the talented and proud drama and art critic from Frankfurt, Germany, Karl Loes. He was embarrassed to ask for help and said that he did not want to become a Christian. But he did become a Christian. He became a powerful leader with university students. When Hitler's armies came to Czechoslovakia, Karl Loes fled for his life and Wallner lost track of him.

At the end of the war, a group of underground fighters were in a cellar. They were all murdered by the Nazis who were leaving in disorganized retreat. On the walls messages were written in various languages. Wallner was asked to translate them. One of the poems he translated read:

> I believe in the sun when it is not shining.
> I believe in love, when I do not feel it.
> I believe in my Lord, Jesus, even when he is silent.[2]

It was signed Karl Loes. Wallner wept at this last tragic meeting with his friend. But there was also gratitude for the faith that had developed to such heights.

THE SYRO-PHOENICIAN WOMAN

The discouragement of the disciples was another attempt to intimidate this woman. They wanted to send her away. She was bothering them. But we cannot send away those that need our help. As Christians, our responsibility is to be sensitive to those who need the help of Christ in ways that we can give it. When those who are closest to Christ send away those who need the help of Christ, where shall they find help? This the woman knew. There was no help elsewhere. The disciples' discouragement was not enough to cause her to go away or to hush her cries.

Neither do we have to be discouraged or intimidated by the methods used by others. There may be ways to bring others to Christ that seem to get more results; but if they are inconsistent with your understanding of the gospel, your approach to persons, or your commitment to Christ, they need not intimidate or discourage you. This woman's method of seeking Christ may have been different from the disciples' methods, but she was not discouraged from acting in faith.

Jesus had a purpose in seeming to intimidate the woman. He reminded her that his purpose was to come to the lost sheep of the house of Israel. But refusing to be intimidated by that more narrowly defined purpose, she still asked him to help her. He had come to the house of Israel, but he had the power to help others who would call upon him. How much she knew about the power of Jesus we do not know. What she had heard or witnessed of his ability to help those who called on him we do not know. But she was able to sense what both the disciples and the religious leaders were very slow to sense: Jesus had a mission and ministry that transcended national, racial, religious, and cultural barriers. Jesus had come to the world. She was claiming that.

I recall a time when we were in Israel and a member of the tour group got sick suddenly. The bus driver remembered a neighborhood medical clinic in the area. Leaving the tour group at the attraction where they were, he took the bus, one of our group leaders, and the sick man and his wife to the clinic. Finding a physician who could speak English, the man was soon treated and returned to the hotel. The group was able to keep its itinerary. Fortunately, this physician did not think that his only purpose was to minister to those of the house of Israel. Neither did the Christ.

We often face the problem of being intimidated by others. Peer pressure or the reaction of others intimidates us many times. This is the very reason that we do not witness more or serve more or discipline children more or show more loyalty to the local church. It is often not that we do not want to do those things, but rather that we are intimidated by how others might react. But to live in faith, we must refuse to be intimidated by others.

Recognition

Recognition is also involved in this demonstration of faith. It is the recognition that we have no claim of God. We live lives of faith when we recognize that we have no claim of God. God acts toward us in love and mercy as an expression of his love and as a demonstration of his grace.

There was a very interesting exchange between Jesus and the woman. After stating his purpose as having been sent to the lost sheep of the house of Israel, Jesus said that one would not feed the children's bread to the dogs. (You might remember that the Jews called the Gentiles dogs.) The woman's reply was that while a loving father would not feed the children's bread to the dogs, the dogs would eat any of the crumbs that fell from the table. Then Jesus complimented her on her faith and healed her daughter. Her faith brought results.

This woman recognized that she had no claim on God. But she was willing to take any of the grace of God that he would bestow on her. She could not claim any prior commitment of God to her. But she would act on the promises of God, as expressed in Jesus Christ. Martin Luther observed that this woman threw the sack of Jesus' promises at his feet.

The only claim that any of us have on God is grace. We can

THE SYRO-PHOENICIAN WOMAN   67

never claim the love of God or the promises of God due to our own merit or our achievement or even our work for him. The only claim that we have is that God acts toward us in grace.

God owes us nothing. We don't have any promissory note that we can cash in on God. What God does for us is the result of his grace.

God acts in his grace to give us salvation and strength. God will truly hear our cries and grant his mercy to us. But it will be because he acts in grace toward us, not because he is somehow obligated to us. We have no claim on God.

David Lockard directs the missionary orientation program of our denomination's Foreign Mission Board. Prior to that he was a missionary in what is now Zimbabwe. In a chapel service Lockard told of heading out into the bush to preach. As most ministers, he was running late. The road was bad and the location was rather isolated. They passed a car that was out of commission parked by the side of the road. Two nationals were standing by the car. As they passed them, Lockard said that he did not recognize either of them as men whom he knew. They discussed whether to stop and thus be later to their appointment or to go on. They decided that they ought to stop since the road was rather isolated and they did not know when other help might come. So they stopped their land rover, backed it up to where the other car was parked, and got out and approached the men. As they approached, they heard one man say to the other, "See, that is our missionary in Gwelo. I knew that he would stop. Our missionary in Gwelo would not pass us up."

Lockard stated that he did not know the man, but the man knew him. He had no claim on him other than the knowledge that he was the missionary from Gwelo. As a missionary he represented the Christ who also helped people who had no claim on him other than his grace.

When we live the life of faith, we recognize that we have no claim on God. But we are also confident that God will act in his gracious mercy to help us when we call on him.

"Great is your faith!" What a one-sentence characterization

of a life that is. It was said to an unnamed woman who called to the Christ from out of the crowd. Trying to escape the crowds, Christ found that one woman who demonstrated faith in her life.

Notes

1. *Time,* "People," Nov. 1, 1971, p. 52. Used by permission.
2. Ken Olson, *Can You Wait Till Friday?* (Waco: Word Books, 1976).

Part III
The Crowd in the City

"Where Cross the Crowded Ways of Life." That is the city. For the people of Jesus' time and place "the city" was Jerusalem. Every time he went to Jerusalem he found people from out of the crowded streets and temple area to whom he related.

9

A Crippled Man: The Compassion of Christ

Jesus Christ introduced a vast new concept into the world, the concept of compassion. Compassion is the ability to suffer with another. Compassion has its root in the worth of the individual.

This concept that started as a spiritual concept is now loose in the world with enough dynamite in it to blast all our social systems to atoms. That is precisely what it has been doing. It clashed with slavery and struck the fetters from the slaves; it is liberating women, throwing protection around children, and building hospitals for the sick. For a long time it has been the indirect impulse, along with other factors, behind the social upsurging of the masses.

But if compassion has its roots in the worth of the individual, it has its expression in the heart of God and through the illustration of Jesus' compassionate concern with the people he met. Whenever Jesus saw human need, he moved with compassion and love to meet that need. This led Frank C. Laubach, that great missionary servant of Christ, to write: "It would be better for us to throw away ninety-nine percent of our learning and of our tangled philosophy and stick to just one simple thing for our daily life—to keep asking God, 'Who needs me next, Father?' "[1]

Jesus illustrated the compassionate heart of God best in his encounter with the crippled man at the pool of Bethesda (John 5:1-18). Jesus was in Jerusalem for an unnamed feast (many expositors think it was a Feast of Pentecost) when he went around by the sheep market to the pool called Bethesda, the house of mercy, which had five porches. Many ailing and infirm people were around this pool because of the tradition that occasionally an angel would stir the water and the first person in the

A CRIPPLED MAN

pool would be healed of his disease.

While walking among these unfortunate people, Jesus came to one friendless, hopeless person who had been ill for thirty-eight years. Instead of the man asking Jesus to heal him, Jesus asked the man if he had a desire to be well. After the man offered his excuse why he was not healed after so long a time, Jesus healed him.

This became the occasion of controversy between Jesus and the Jewish leaders that ultimately brought about his death. The controversy began because Jesus had healed the man on the sabbath. They had found the man carrying his pallet. He referred them to Jesus, the one who had healed him, thinking that if one could heal of illness he surely should be obeyed when he told someone to pick up his bed, even if it were the sabbath. But when the Jewish leaders talked to Jesus, the problem was compounded. Not only did Jesus admit to healing on the sabbath but he also claimed an equality with God. He said that God continued to work in his providential care of the world on the sabbath and that he could work too. From that point on, we are told, the Jews sought to kill Jesus.

Now what new concept of God was revealed to men by this sign? That God is a God of compassion and mercy.

Christ brings compassion. The Jewish leaders were convinced that God was a God of legalism—that he was most interested in one keeping the sabbath law. Jesus showed that God is a God of compassion. He is more interested in meeting human need and healing a broken, disappointed, friendless man.

Someone has said that the most heretical idea is that God is primarily interested in religion. God is not just interested in religious observance. This was the heresy into which the Jewish leaders had fallen. They thought that God was primarily interested in a person keeping the sabbath law. Jesus showed that God was primarily interested in helping persons.

Truly, Christ brings compassion. Christ shows us that compassion is the expression of the heart of God. Jesus illustrated this compassion in his own life. From the crowd around the pool of Bethesda, Christ touched a man's life.

Choice

In the compassion of Christ, we see God's choice. The first thing we realize in dealing with God is that he takes the initiative. In the other signs, or miracles, in the Gospel of John, Jesus moved in response to a request—his mother's at Cana, the nobleman's when the boy was healed. But here Jesus took the initiative, made the choice. In all of God's working with us, this is the valid principle we must ever keep in mind. We have salvation, healing, power, life because God has made a choice.

When God makes this choice, we are faced with an important question, "Wilt thou be made whole?" On the surface, we would quickly answer, "Yes, I would give anything to be healed." But when we examine our hearts more closely, we may discover that this is not always the case.

Any psychologist will tell us that many people are ill because they want to be ill. Leslie Weatherhead in *Psychology, Religion, and Healing* quoted a case like that. A girl named Kathleen G. was healthy and about twenty. She was a typist in a village garage. She became engaged to the curate of the village and was radiantly happy. A good part of her happiness came from the fact that she was no longer going to be a typist who did not matter in a menial and unimportant job; she was going to be someone of social importance and standing in the neighborhood.

The curate broke off the engagement. From that day, Kathleen developed certain symptoms. She refused to eat. She would even put food into her mouth and then put it out into her handkerchief, hide it away, and destroy it later. She became pale, thin, hollow-eyed, anemic.

She was taken to the doctor, and all that the doctor could say to her parents was, "You must make her eat." She was taken to a specialist. All that he could say was that there was nothing in the world the matter with her and that she must be forced to eat. In desperation, her parents at last took her to Leslie Weatherhead to see if he could treat her by psychological methods. By this time, Kathleen weighed only seventy-three pounds and looked like an Indian famine victim. All she could say was that

A CRIPPLED MAN

she knew that she ought to eat, but an inward power was forbidding her to eat.

Under psychological treatment, her trouble became clear. Unconsciously she wanted to starve to death. To be ill was to have real prominence and not to sink back into the obscurity of being a typist in a village garage. To be ill was to command sympathy. To be ill and to die was to have her revenge on the specialist who said that there was nothing wrong with her. Above all it was to have her revenge on the curate; it was to make him wretched. If she died, she was fairly certain that he would feel responsible for her death.

She was ill for no other reason than that she wanted to be ill. She could not be cured because subconsciously she did not want to be made well. Fortunately psychological treatment was able to reveal the truth to her and to cure her. But as long as she wanted to be ill, nothing on earth could have cured her.

We can often see this kind of thing happening very simply. On the morning of an examination, or before some engagement which we do not wish to face or to fulfill, we develop headaches or colds. We are ill for no other reason than we want to be ill. Illness can be an escape; it can be something through which we evade our responsibilities and through which we avoid the duties we do not want to face. Illness can make us the center of attention. It can bring us sympathy that otherwise we would not have received. To be well, the first essential is to want to be well. To achieve anything, to attain anything, to receive anything, the first essential is to desire it. Jesus' question to the man was by no means superfluous. It went straight to the heart of the matter.

The same is true with our moral and spiritual life. It makes demands upon us. To be forgiven—we must be forgiving. To gain new life—we must live that life in faith. To have control over hatred, fear, temptation—we must show love, faith, power.

But we are made to realize that nothing is impossible with God. This man had been ill for thirty-eight years. This probably seemed to him to be an endless process. But with God, nothing is incurable, nothing is impossible. No habit, no frame of mind, no type of life is beyond the cure of the Christ.

Command

After Jesus asked the question of desire, "Wilt thou be made whole?" he gave a command. Jesus approaches us first at the level of desire. Do you really want forgiveness of sin? Do you really want power over your life? He then moves on to the definite command. The command is threefold.

Jesus commands us to do the thing we cannot do. "Rise," he told the man. It may seem that what Jesus commands of us is expressly the thing we cannot do: love, have control over self and desires and lusts, have faith. But this is exactly what he commands.

Jesus commands us to make no provisions for relapse. "Take up thy bed, and walk," gives no provision for relapse. We must realize that faith is not a provisional thing. When we begin to follow Christ by faith, we can make no provision for relapse.

Jesus commands us to continue in strength. "Walk" was the command of Jesus to the man. He was not to expect to be carried. He would have to move out in strength that would be gained from walking. Only by stretching our spiritual muscles and serving God can we gain the strength for greater service and life.

Concern

When Jesus saw the man again, he showed his real concern. His real concern was for the moral and spiritual life of the man. "Sin no more," was his command this time. This does not indicate that the man's illness was due to his sin. Evidently the matter of the forgiveness of his sin to this point had been handled by Christ. But Christ does show that his primary concern is that the man's whole life show the result of his encounter with Christ.

Christ is concerned that we show through lives of faith and strength, rather than sin, that we have met him.

Many exciting stories of people who have shown this complete change have come out of the Billy Graham crusades. In 1959, Graham conducted a crusade in Melbourne, Australia. The meetings were held in the Sidney Myer Music Bowl. The message reached many of the people of Melbourne, including the irreligious, such as the George Jacksons. Their marriage was breaking down—night clubs, racing, and alcohol were not able to disguise their incompatibility. The husband, who was a former prisoner of war and a foreman in a clothing factory, was alternately violent and moody, refusing for days to speak to his wife and daughters. Jackson was a confidence man as well as a gambler and a blasphemer. Inwardly he knew such misery that he actually wished he could be back in the Japanese camps on the Death Railway—"that I might hide myself away and die in a wallow of self-pity." When the crusade began, George was so incensed by the publicity, so convinced that Graham was "out to make fast money with a good gimmick," that he wrote and told him to "get out of the country."

The Jacksons denied God's existence, but the wife, Dawn, went to the first night of the crusade—"a completley new experience for someone of my background. Yet I dared there to believe that Jesus was a real person and could change my then miserable life." George was amazed when Dawn told him that she had been converted, but he could not deny the change in her life. He said, "She had what I had always wanted, peace of mind." He continued to sneer and refused to go to the crusade, "until I thought I had saved enough face." He then went wearing dark glasses.

In 1965, the Jacksons sailed to Borneo as missionaries.[2]

This is the real concern of Christ for our lives—that our lives be changed by an encounter with him. The lame man had known nothing but disappointment and defeat in his life. After he met Christ, he knew forgiveness and personal power and meaning. This can be our experience.

Christ, indeed, brings compassion. In this, he showed us that God was more interested in persons than in principles. God is that interested in us.

Notes

1. Quoted in William Barclay, *And He Had Compassion On Them* (Edinburgh: The Church of Scotland Youth Committee, 1955), p. 191.
2. John Pollock, *Billy Graham The Authorized Biography* (New York: McGraw-Hill Book Company, 1966), pp. 192-193.

10

A Blind Man: The Light from Christ

In Joseph Haydn's oratorio, *the Creation*, the passage where the words "And there was light" occur is very significant. The first three words are sung moderately, but at the word "light" the orchestra and choir burst forth fortissimo, in a wild transport of ecstacy. It is as if all the suns and lights in the cosmos blazed up at one stroke, like a fountain of light ascending to the heavens. Everything is now different, for light has come into the world.

Anyone who has ever spent the night beside the bed of a sick loved one, thinking that perhaps the next breath would be the last, knows something of the sense of relief and expectancy that comes with the dawn. Light has come into the world, everything seems brighter!

In the creation account, the Scripture records, "God saw the light, that it was good" (Gen. 1:4). Indeed, it is good for light to be in the world.

As Christ brought to us the final and complete revelation of God, he brought light into the world. *Light* is one of the key words in the Gospel of John. Twice in the space of two chapters Jesus made the claim for himself, "I am the light of the world" (John 8:12; 9:5). This is exactly the function that Jesus performs in his ministry in the world. Light dispels darkness. Light reveals. Light penetrates. Light illuminates. All of these things are the things that Jesus does in our lives. He drives the darkness of sin from our lives. He reveals the wonders and greatness of God to us. He penetrates into the innermost portions of our lives and activities. He illuminates life with meaning and purpose.

Jesus first made this startling claim at a Feast of the Tabernacles. On the first night of the feast, four candelabra were placed in the Court of the Women and with the coming of night were lighted to illumine every part of that court. The candelabra signified the pillar of fire with which God had guided his people during the wilderness wanderings. Jesus then proclaimed that this light burned brightly for awhile, then was extinguished; but he would be the light that lasts forever, lighting the dark places in the hearts of men and lighting the pathway which they would follow.

The second time Jesus made this claim was when the man blind from birth was given sight. Jesus demonstrated his claim by giving sight to the man. Not only did he claim to bring light into the world but also he demonstrated his ability to do so by giving sight to the man who had been deprived of light all of his life. In the crowd around Christ was one man who could not see. Jesus gave him sight; Jesus gave him light. The incident is found in John 9:1-12.

This act engaged Jesus in controversy with the Jewish leaders. He had done it on a sabbath. By working and by healing, he had broken the sabbath. To make matters worse, he had done an unheard of thing—healing a man of congenital blindness. The Pharisees questioned the man, his parents, and later Jesus himself. Jesus made good his claim to be the Light of the world.

Jesus makes good his claim to be the Light of the world. Today his function as the Light of the world is the same as it was then—to drive darkness from human hearts and minds. How is this done? How does Christ bring light to this generation that considers itself more enlightened than any other group of people?

Light to Darkened Ideas About Suffering

Christ brings light to darkened ideas about suffering. The occasion of this miracle was the question of the disciples about the source of the man's blindness. Since the disciples connected suffering with sin, thinking it impossible for a person to suffer without having sinned and that suffering was payment for sin, they asked Jesus, "Who sinned, this man or his parents, that he was born blind?" (John 9:2).

A BLIND MAN

There is evidence that the Jews had a belief that sin influenced a child while it was still in its mother's womb. There is medical evidence today that children may suffer prenatally as the direct result of their parents' wrongdoing. But it is not correct always to connect each situation of suffering with a specific sin. Jesus' answer indicated that in this instance the man's suffering was not the result of his sin. His suffering, rather, would result in the glory of God. H. E. Dana made a good statement at this point. He said, "Suffering should not become an occasion for doubt and controversy, but should be turned into a means of glorifying God and more effectively performing his work on earth."[1]

This is unbelievable, we say. How can suffering result in the glory of God?

Suffering can result in the glory of God by demonstrating how Christians react to suffering. Anyone can serve God when things are going well and no demands are made on the faith and strength of an individual. But when suffering strikes, it often becomes harder to serve God and to witness by one's life. However, one of the strongest witnesses given to the power of God is that which has come out of the suffering of God's children. William Barclay tells of an old saint who was dying in an agony of pain. He sent for his family, saying, "Come and see how a Christian can die."[2] By the way in which we Christians bear suffering, we can demonstrate what God can do for us.

One of the most thrilling and familiar stories of martyrdom, the martyrdom of Polycarp, bishop of Smyrna, illustrates this truth. In the middle of the second century, during the annual festival of Caesar in Smyrna, Polycarp was seized by the Roman authorities. Even some of the officials tried to persuade Polycarp to recant and to say, "Caesar is Lord." But the old man staunchly refused. When he had entered the arena, the proconsul told him, "Swear, and I will release thee; blaspheme Christ." To this Polycarp replied, "Eighty and six years have I served Christ, and he has never done me wrong. How can I blaspheme my king, who saved me?"

After passing judgment on Polycarp, they were about to nail him to the stake to burn him. He said to them, "Leave me as I am, for he that hath granted me to endure the fire will grant me also to endure the pile unmoved, even without the security that ye seek from the nails." So they did not nail him, but tied him to the stake. Then Polycarp offered his last prayer: "O Lord God Almighty, the Father of Thy well-beloved and ever-blessed Son, Jesus Christ, by whom we have received the knowledge of Thee, . . . I thank Thee that Thou hast graciously thought me worthy of this day and of this hour, that I may receive a portion among the number of martyrs, in the cup of Thy Christ."[3] Polycarp demonstrated the power of God. Suffering, in this case, resulted in the glory of God by demonstrating how Christians react to suffering.

Suffering can result in the glory of God by demonstrating how Christians react to the suffering of others. Jesus has been called "the man for others." If Christians identify with Jesus in this intense care and concern for others, it will be seen in the way they react to the suffering of other people. When Christians are moved by the suffering of others to act for them and to seek to minister to them in the name of the Lord Jesus Christ, then glory to God is a result of their reactions.

Of course, the most engaging example at this point is that of Albert Schweitzer. He could have chosen a career as a minister, a theological professor, a musician, or a surgeon in his native Alsace-Lorraine. Instead, he chose to identify himself with suffering humanity and serve as a jungle doctor in Africa. He explained his action by saying, "It struck me as incomprehensible that I should be allowed to lead such a happy life, while I saw so many people around me wrestling with care and suffering."[4]

Our problem is that we see some of these people wrestling with care and suffering but we react with selfishness rather than selflessness. People watch the way Christians react to the sufferings of others. Therefore, Christians must be sure to react to the sufferings of others with the compassionate concern of the Christ so that God's glory will be demonstrated.

This man's suffering was not caused just for the purpose of Jesus working a miracle and thus bringing glory to God. Rather, by the suffering of this man, Jesus was able to relieve suffering and bring glory to God. In the process, Jesus brought light to some darkened ideas about suffering.

Light to Darkened Ideas About Self

In this Scripture passage, we see some ideas about self that need enlightening.

One thing we see is that Christ moves to act when we realize our need of him. This blind man realized his need. His need was apparent to all who saw him. Jesus knew he was breaking the sabbath law when he healed the man. But, to him, as it ought to be with us, people were more important than principles. To the Pharisees when they questioned him, the man gave one of the most eloquent testimonies of Christian faith: "One thing I know, that, whereas I was blind, now I see" (9:25). The most effective Christian witness we can give is to our own experiences of realizing our needs and how Jesus Christ met those needs.

One of the memories of my Baptist deacon father that I will cherish as long as I live is that of sitting in a darkened car in the driveway after returning home from a football game. In very simple terms my father explained his own experience of salvation to an unsaved neighbor. No sermon can be quite so eloquent as the testimony of a person who can say to a friend, "One thing I know, that, whereas I was blind, now I see."

Another idea about self that is revealed here is that self-deception can keep us from seeing our need. This deception may come from fear. This was true of the parents of the man who had been healed. Because they were afraid of the consequences, they would not bear a clear witness to Christ. Fear of what we may find keeps many of us from really trying to know ourselves and admit our needs.

Self-deception can come from pride or arrogance. This was the problem with the Pharisees in verses 39-41. As long as our pride and arrogance keep us from admitting our need of Christ and his saving power, Christ can do nothing for us. Jesus indicated that this refusal to see ourselves as sinners heightens our guilt.

Light to Darkened Ideas About Salvation

From the rapidly moving events of this story, we can see a concept of salvation that is important for us to comprehend. A progression of understanding on the part of this man who was healed illustrates something of the progression of faith that brings salvation.

Faith begins with the understanding that Jesus Christ can meet our needs. In the first interview with the people, all the healed man knew was that Jesus had healed him. He didn't know who Jesus was or how he went about healing. In order to accept salvation, we must first be convinced that Jesus can bring us salvation.

Faith progresses to the realization that Jesus brings to us the power and word of God. The healed man called Jesus a prophet when he talked with the Pharisees. A prophet brings the words and thoughts of God to men. Through Jesus, we see God's power and God's words revealed in a remarkable way.

Faith reaches full bloom with the confession of Christ as the Son of God. After the man had been cast out of the Temple, Jesus sought him. Jesus spoke to him, and the man discovered that Jesus was the Son of God. It is not until we confess Jesus as the Son of God and the Lord of life that faith becomes complete and salvation becomes a reality. Once Napoleon was in a group of skeptics who were talking about Jesus. They dismissed Jesus as one of the world's greatest men. "Gentlemen," said Napoleon, "I know men, and Jesus Christ is more than a man." As the man who had been healed came to know more about Jesus, he ranked him higher. And so will we.

Many people have some darkened ideas about salvation. Some think that salvation comes by membership in a certain church. Others think that salvation is a rather automatic process that comes through being morally good or from having Christian parents. Some think salvation comes from assent to some formula for salvation. Others think that salvation is a process of self-realization, that all people will ultimately be saved. To these darkened ideas of salvation comes the light of Christ telling us that salvation is a personal relationship with Jesus Christ. It is a relationship that is established when we are able, through faith, to confess Jesus as the Son of God and commit our lives to him in complete faith.

Jesus brought light to the man born blind. Jesus is able to bring light to us today. Many of us, like the Pharisees, do not realize that we need light. But as we recognize our need and turn our lives to Christ, we can see that he brings light to our darkened ideas about suffering, self, and salvation.

Notes

1. H. E. Dana, *The Heavenly Guest* (Nashville: Broadman Press, 1943), p. 84.
2. William Barclay, *The Gospel of John, II* (Philadelphia: The Westminster Press, 1958), p. 46.
3. Herbert B. Workman, *Persecution in the Early Church* (New York and Nashville: Abingdon Press, 1960. Apex Books edition), pp. 134-136.
4. Albert Schweitzer, *Out of My Life and Thought* (New York: Mentor Books, 1953), pp. 69-70.

11

A Lawyer: The Commandment to Love

We are creatures of law. If asked, most of us would answer that we are completely law-abiding. Yet at the same time that the assertion is made, there is also the realization that it is not absolutely true. We have broken some laws, whether consciously or unconsciously. We are literally hedged about with laws. Take our automobiles, for instance. We have laws that tell us we can drive a car, where to drive that car, and even how to drive it. In almost every activity of the human endeavor, we can find some law to help us regulate our activities. Which of these laws is the most important? Which law stands out above all others to be obeyed whether others are ignored?

This was exactly the question that a lawyer asked Jesus one day. That was a day of questions for the Christ. A Herodian had asked him a political question. A Sadducee had asked him a theological question. And now a Pharisee asked him a legal question (see Mark 12:28-34; Matt. 22:34-40).

This was a very live issue. There were two tendencies in Judaism concerning the law. One was to expand the law limitlessly. The Pharisees had come up with six hundred and thirteen laws based on the commandments of God and their interpretations of them. The other tendency was to try to gather up the law in one sentence or general statement. William Barclay related that the great rabbi Hillel was once asked by a proselyte to instruct him in the whole law while he stood on one leg. Hillel's answer was that what he hated for himself do not for his neighbor. That was the whole law, the rest was commentary. Then he suggested that he go learn it.

When asked this question by the shrewd lawyer, Jesus joined two of the old Jewish laws to form his answer. The first part of

> # A LAWYER

the answer indicated that there is but one God, and we should love him supremely (Deut. 6:4-9). But to this Jesus added a second part: that we should love our neighbor as ourselves (Lev. 19:18). No rabbi or any other teacher had made this union before. In doing this, Jesus was saying that the heart of religion is not seen in negative commands but in a positive attitude toward God and man.

The lawyer did not ask this question for information. Matthew's account makes it plain that the lawyer was trying to test Jesus by the question. All of the questions in that day had been for the purpose of trapping Jesus. But after this particular question and Jesus' answer to it, Mark observed, "And after that no one dared to ask him any question" (Mark 12:34, RSV).

From out of the crowd came a lawyer with a question to trap Jesus. But Jesus turned the question to a positive teaching. He gave us the commandment to love. An authority in the law should have known the law. But Jesus carried the lawyer right to the center of the law. This man's identity will always remain unknown to us. Who he was is not really as important as what he was—an authority on the law who tried to trip Jesus up with the law—and what Jesus did with his question. For us, as for the first-century Jew, the most important law deals with our relationship with God and, growing out of that, our relationship to our fellowman. The great commandment is rooted in God and reaches toward man. We have a commandment to love.

Answer

Jesus prefaced his answer with the quotation of the Shema (Deut. 6:4-9). This is the capstone of the Jewish faith. The Hebrews were commanded to wear this statement in little leather boxes called phylacteries which they wore on their arms and their foreheads at times. They put it in little cylindrical boxes on both sides of all the doors of their homes so they could be reminded of it everytime they went in or out. They quoted it at the beginning of each synagogue service. This is the most important fact of all Judaism: The Lord is one God. The great commandment begins with God. We have only one God.

How truthful are we when we say this? The ancients were very truthful about their gods. They gave them names and personalities and worshiped them openly. We have repudiated Zeus, Venus, Aretemus, and Bacchus; but, in our sophistication and search for meaning, we have added other gods. These new false gods are just as real and demand just as much from us in interest and service. We may call them science, humanism, individualism, politics, pleasure, work, or sex. But these are the things that many moderns exalt.

The Old Testament called this idolatry. The prophets said that the relationship to God is such that when his people run after false gods they have committed spiritual adultery. One sage once observed that a person does not have to confine himself to a single god. But the person who divides his loyalty splits himself. He is no longer integrated about a single center, so his personality becomes equivocal and ambiguous. In its extreme form, this phenomenon is known clinically as schizophrenia. In biblical terms, its diagnosis is polytheism.

But there can also be the matter of claiming to believe in God but in living as though God did not exist. These are the people that J. Wallace Hamilton labeled as the real atheists of any age. He asserted that the people who call themselves atheists are monotonous but mostly harmless. The real atheists are those who have some vague idea of God—one who lived long ago and does not live now and work and move among us.

We can find God in his love for us. Jesus could have been indicating to the lawyer that he knew the answer to his question. It was written on his wrist. There is one God and this God loves us. When we have found God, we have found love. Count Leo Tolstoy could have been described as the man who had everything: the title of nobility, lands, money, talent for writing. He had tried every way he knew to find meaning in life. But he had not succeeded until one day in the forest he met a peasant who had nothing but black bread to eat. But this peasant was so evidently full of serenity and joy that Tolstoy asked him what made him so happy. He replied that he had bread to eat that Tolstoy knew not of: the Bread of life. He then advised the count to find

God and he would have it. Tolstoy persisted until he had an experience with God. He afterwards described the experience as having filled him with joyous waves of light and which wrought in him a profound and lasting change. Tolstoy asserted that to know God is to live.

We begin to comprehend the great commandment, the commandment to love, when we know that there is one God and that he loves us.

Attitude

Since we have one God and he loves us, what is our attitude toward him? We are to love him. We are to love the God who loved us so much. Jesus said, "Thou shalt love the Lord thy God with all thy heart, and with all thy soul, and with all thy mind, and with all thy strength" (Mark 12:30). This means that we are to love God with all the faculties of our lives. He has shown his love to us. He has sought us when we were unlovely. He has given his Son, Jesus Christ, to die on the cross for us.

We have come to God through his love for us. The great truth of God's love is that he loves us and cares for us. Toyohiko Kagawa, one of the religious leaders of Japan of a past generation, said that God came to him in an isolated hut along the seaside. Stricken with tuberculosis as a young man, he was separated from even his own people. One day a Christian missionary came to him with food and medicine. After the missionary left, Kagawa asked himself why a stranger who was not even one of his own countrymen would bother with him. The only answer that he could get was that God was in that man. Once young Kagawa asked the missionary if he were not afraid of him. The missionary's answer was that although Kagawa's disease was contagious, love was more contagious. It was through love that Kagawa came to Christ.

We then express this love to God. To love God supremely is to be dedicated to him completely. This love is the motivation for service and ministry. The love that we have for God is what sends us out in ministry to the people who need the love of God. The Great Commission would have little force for us were it not for the Great Commandment upon which it rests.

The love of God is not selfish. All that we know of God's love through Christ assures us of that. If it had been selfish, Christ would have preserved his life rather than have sacrificed his life. We cannot be selfish with it either. If we have experienced the love of God, we are to express the love of God. The experience of the love of God without the expression of the love of God is not the proper Christian order.

This love of God is what draws us together. Years ago George W. Truett, in *Follow Thou Me*, wrote about an old man gazing earnestly at a picture of the thorn-crowned Christ in a well-known art gallery. As he looked at the painting, the expression involuntarily broke from his lips, "Bless him! I love him!" A stranger who was standing nearby heard the old man's words and clasped his hands to say, "Brother, I love him too." And then they were joined by a third person, a fourth person, and others who had been strangers to one another before but who were brought together by a common love for the crucified Lord.

The commandment to love given to that lawyer from out of the crowd in the city focuses around the God of love whom we are to love supremely.

Action

But Jesus did not stop where so many of us want to stop: with our relationship of love to God. He went on to tie that into our relationship with humankind. Jesus assured us that we cannot love God without loving persons also. This love reaches out to serve God by serving other persons. This is a practical kind of love, not just a sentimental feeling.

The commandment to love goes from an attitude of love to the action of love. Real love always acts. It always acts in real, tangible ways that affect people. This is the practical side of Christianity—Christianity in action. After we discover the nature of God, after we have ascertained the authority of the Bible, we see that Christianity has a practical side that issues in action. After we recognize the reality of sin, after we have experienced the wonder of redemption, after we have become a part

A LAWYER

of the church of Christ, we see the practical side of Christianity. Our doctrine does us no good if it does not issue in action. Our doctrine does us no good if it does not issue in practical help. If our doctrine does not thrust us out of the church into the world to make the love of Christ known, there is something wrong with it. Here we meet the lonely, the disenchanted, the sorrowing, the hurt, those who have a definite heart need. We must not just have pity, but the type of love that will move us to action to show the attitude of Christ in helping the helpless.

In the experience recorded in Luke, the lawyer who asked the question of Jesus tried to justify himself by asking another question: "Who is my neighbor?" (Luke 10:29). In answering that question, Jesus gave us one of his most memorable stories: the parable of the good Samaritan. By this answer, Jesus showed us that the question is usually asked improperly. It is not, "Who is my neighbor?" but, "To whom am I a neighbor?"

The story Jesus told could well have actually occurred. The road from Jerusalem to Jericho dropped thirty-six hundred feet in a little more than twenty miles. It had sharp curves and blind corners. It seemed made to order for the robbers who used it.

Probably the traveler who went alone on the road was somewhat foolhardy, but nevertheless he had fallen among the thieves. They had badly beaten him and robbed him. A priest came along. The priest took one look at the man and then tried to divert his eyes, as though he did not see him as he walked by on the other side. This may have been the priest's week to serve in the Temple, and he did not want to defile himself with the possibility of touching a dead body. Then the Levite came along.

Levites were also Temple servants. Apparently the Levite came over and looked at him but likely thinking that he was a decoy he, too, hurried by on the other side. Then came a Samaritan. He may have been a Samaritan by race or he may have been such an irreligious, unorthodox person that he was called a Samaritan as a term of contempt. Remember that Jesus was even called a Samaritan once. The people who represented the ones organized to do good passed him by. The one from whom no good was expected did the deed of mercy and goodness. The reversal of the question is the whole point of the parable: To whom am I a neighbor?

The person to whom we are to be a neighbor is the person who needs help. When we love our neighbors as ourselves, we begin to see that.

We can be perfectly logical in our thinking and still wind up with the wrong answer about our neighbor. The person who is asked for help and the person who needs the help may have different ideas about the definition of *neighbor*. For instance, the man applying for a job may have lost his job due to changing technology. He thinks the other man ought to have a job for him because he has a business. But the person to whom he applies for the job may think that he would already have a job if he were willing to work. Both might have perfectly logical answers, but wrong. Our neighbor is the person in need whom we can help.

Without doubt all those who passed the man by had pity on him. But only the Samaritan had the pity that issued in help

Someone produced a parable which tried to make clear the different attitudes of the founders of the great religions to a man in trouble. A man had fallen into a pit and could not get out. Buddha passed by. He observed that the man must have been a very foolish fellow to get into a mess like that. But he could do nothing to help him. Mohammed passed by. He said that he was very sorry that he could not get the man out of the pit; but if he ever did get out Mohammed would give the man some rules and regulations that would keep him from falling in again. Jesus of Nazareth passed by. He said nothing but got down into the pit and lifted the man out.

The commandment to love is the commandment that issues in action. Love makes itself known to other people.

The lawyer was in the crowd when he asked the question. His motive was to trap Jesus. How could one determine which of the many commandments was the greatest? But Jesus' answer struck right to the heart of religion. The commandment to love rests on the one God who loves us and whom we love by loving him and loving other persons. Love always makes itself known.

12

Mary of Bethany: The Extravagance of Love

"The Gift of the Magi" by O. Henry is one of my favorite short stories. Della and Jim were a young couple who were very poor but very much in love. Each had one unique possession. Della's hair was her glory. When she let it down, it almost served as a robe. Jim had a gold watch, his pride, which had come to him from his father.

On the day before Christmas, Della had exactly one dollar eighty-seven cents with which to buy Jim a present. She did the only thing she could do: She went out and sold her hair for twenty dollars. With the proceeds, she bought a platinum fob for Jim's precious watch.

Jim came home from work that night. When he saw Della's shorn head, he stopped as if stupified. It was not that he did not like it or love her any more. She was lovelier than ever. Slowly he handed her his gift. His gift was a set of expensive tortoise-shell combs with jewelled edges for her lovely hair. He had sold his gold watch to buy them for her. Each had given all he or she had to give. Very clearly, love was extravagant in its actions.

The dominant feeling we get when we read the account of the anointing of Jesus with precious ointment by Mary of Bethany is the extravagance of love. Love is extravagant.

This event occurred in the last week of the Lord's earthly life. He had gone to Bethany where a meal was given in his honor at the home of Simon the Leper. Bethany was a suburb of the city of Jerusalem.

We are not sure of the identity of Simon the Leper. Since Mary, Martha, and Lazarus were there, some have thought that he was their father. It is not too much to suppose that Simon the Leper was a leper who had been healed by Jesus.

Neither Mark (14:3-9) nor Matthew (26:6-13) identified the woman who anointed Jesus with the ointment. Something else that must be noted is that both Mark and Matthew indicate that it was Jesus' head she anointed. John states that Mary anointed Jesus' feet (12:3). At any rate, at a meal given in Jesus' honor, possibly at the home of a person who had received God's gift of healing through Jesus, an act of extravagant love was performed. This is also understood as a different event from the sinful woman who anointed Jesus' feet and wiped them dry with her hair (Luke 7:36-50). The event we're concerned with is set in the shadow of the cross and is related to the death of Jesus.

John's Gospel identifies the woman who anointed Jesus as Mary of Bethany (12:2-8). This is the same Mary who was, at another time, reprimanded by her sister, Martha, for sitting at Jesus' feet listening to him instead of helping with the meal. This Mary is the sister of Lazarus whom Jesus raised from the dead. In fact, John's account indicated that Lazarus was at the meal. This family was especially close to Jesus. He loved them; and they loved him. In one of his last times of friendship and fellowship before the ordeal of the cross, Jesus relaxed with friends. Out of all the crowds that hovered around Jesus, this family was chosen as friends. From this crowd came one person—Mary—to show an act of extravagant love. But then that is the nature of love: Love is always extravagant. Love caused Jesus to give his life for us. While Mary's action in expressing her love to Jesus seems extravagant, it certainly expressed the message of intense love for Jesus.

Objective

The objective of extravagant love is to express itself to the loved one without counting the cost. Love never counts the cost. Mary of Bethany did not count the cost of her gift to Jesus. She gave it out of love.

No parent reminds his child how many times he has gotten up on a cold night to tuck him in, how many pairs of scuffed shoes he has replaced, how often he has done without for him. No wife has added up the total of dishes washed, socks mended, or floors swept. True love never counts the cost.

So it ought to be with our service to God in love. What it might cost us really doesn't make much difference. The important thing is that we have the heart and the love to express our feelings to God in service and devotion.

In that chapter of the New Testament we call the "Love Chapter," 1 Corinthians 13, Paul made that clear. First Corinthians 13:5 states that love "seeketh not her own." Or as *The New English Bible* translates 13:6, "Love keeps no score of wrongs; does not gloat over other men's sins, but delights in truth." J. B. Phillips in *The New Testament in Modern English* translates verse 5, "Love has good manners and does not pursue selfish advantage."

Do you think Jesus ever sat down to count what it would cost him to save you? Surely, he realized it. But love was so strong that all of this was pushed aside to die for us. Philippians 2:5-8 expresses this so well, "Christ Jesus . . . did not count equality with God a thing to be grasped, but emptied himself . . . humbled himself and became obedient unto death, even death on a cross" (RSV). This thought must be uppermost in our minds whenever we think of the cost of following Jesus.

This must also be our attitude to service for Christ. Baker James Cauthen, former executive secretary of the Foreign Mission Board of the Southern Baptist Convention, was once asked the question of how much it cost to win just one person to Christ on a foreign mission field. Cauthen's answer was superb. He said that if we divide the number of dollars by the number of baptisms on the mission fields we would get only a fragmentary picture of what is done. The cost in terms of steadfastness, longsuffering, and dedicated service of the missionaries could never be measured in any kind of terms. Love doesn't count the cost of service to God.

The objective of Mary's loving act was Jesus. She directed her love to him. But what if that love were never expressed? Nathaniel Hawthorne wrote one of the greatest novels in American literature in his notable work, *The Scarlet Letter*. This book probably would never have been written if it had not been for the love expressed by his wife when he needed her most.

Hawthorne lost his job and came home in deep despair. With understanding, patience, faith, and love, his wife encouraged him to use the time he now had to write the book he had wanted to write. The love of his thoughtful wife sent Hawthorne forward to discover his better self.

In gratitude, Hawthorne wrote to his wife, Sophia, that she only had taught him that he had a heart; that she only had thrown a light downward and upward into his soul and had revealed him to himself. Without her aid, he said, his best knowledge of himself would have been merely to know his own shadow, to watch it flickering on a wall, and to mistake its fantasies for his own real actions.

But what if Sophia had never expressed her love? Would Hawthorne have ever been able to produce the literature that has remained for all these years? Mary loved Jesus with an extravagant love. But what if she had never expressed that love? He could have gone to his cross without knowing the extent of her love for him. And what if you never express your love to Jesus? What has gone undone in the kingdom of God because you have counted the cost rather than expressed an act of love to the Savior?

Opportunity

Love always takes the opportunity to act. One of our greatest failures is that we do not take the opportunity to serve. Jesus said a cup of cold water given in his name has meaning. So many little expressions of love and appreciation would mean so much if we would just take the opportunity to express them: a kind word of encouragement; a pat on the back; the assurance of your prayers; a letter of appreciation; the affirmation of a person. In all of these ways, we can show ordinary love, not even extravagant love, to others if we would but take the opportunity to do it. Do it now! is one message from this event.

MARY OF BETHANY

Mary of Bethany seized the opportunity to express love to Jesus. Jesus recognized it as an act of the anointing of his body for burial when he could still appreciate it. The day would come when she could no longer show that kind of regard for him with his knowledge of it. At this time, he knew it and acknowledged it. Mary loved Jesus and took the opportunity to express it with an act of extravagant love.

What Mary did was impulsive. There come times when we can't just sit back and think of all the angles before we do something. The very impulsiveness of the act is the thing that caught the disciples off guard and caused them to murmur at what Mary had done. But at the same time, acts of love can be very impulsive. Take that opportunity to act for God when it is presented to you. You may not have that opportunity again. Anyone can do what is expected of him. When we do the unexpected in love, the act becomes significant.

A biblical example of a person missing an opportunity is Felix, the Roman governor, as Paul stood before him. Felix trembled after Paul had reasoned of righteousness, temperance, and judgment to come. Then Felix said, "Go thy way for this time; when I have a convenient season I will call for thee" (Acts 24:25). As far as we know, Felix never had a convenient season.

You may never have another opportunity to do what you know Christ wants you to do in mission, ministry, and witness. Extravagant love takes the opportunity to express itself. Years ago I heard Roy O. McClain tell of some paratroopers who dropped behind the German lines before D day in World War II. One of them fell in a French farm yard. He asked the farm family to hide him. They hid him in the woodbox. The German soldiers came. In searching the house, they found the paratrooper hiding in the woodbox. They killed the husband in the home. The paratrooper later escaped from the German soldiers. Returning to the farm house he once again asked the farm wife to hide him. The woman hid him in the woodbox again. The German soldiers also returned to the house and searched the house again. But this time they did not examine the woodbox. He was safe. Love took the opportunity to express itself even at great cost. That is the nature of extravagant love.

Observance

Through this act of extravagant love, Mary of Bethany set up a memorial to the Master that has been observed ever since. Each act of extravagant love performed for the Savior is an observance of this memorial of love.

The disciples could only think of the cost of the gift. The ointment cost about the average annual wage of a working man. But Jesus was thinking of the motive behind the gift.

With Judas' warped mind, all he could consider was the cost. This warped view of life puts a monetary value on everything and every act and never goes beyond the dollar sign. Love can never be measured in monetary terms. This woman loved Jesus so much that she was willing to give him the most valuable thing that she had.

Jesus praised Mary for her gift. She was anointing his body for burial even before the time of burial. Jesus commended her on her insight that his way was the way of death. Some things can be done at almost any time. Other things will never be done unless the moment is grasped at which they can be done. Money could be given to the poor at any time. The memorial to the life and death of the Master could only be observed at that time. Mary could have helped the poor at any time; Judas could have helped them at any time too if that were what he really wanted. But it was only at this time that the heart's devotion to Jesus could be done before the cross on Calvary took him into its cruel arms.

Had that money been spent on the poor, it would soon have been forgotten—by the poor and by the disciples. We would never have heard of it. But since the money was spent as an expression of love, whenever we think of the price of love our thoughts are drawn to this gift. It can never be forgotten. It always stands as a memorial to love.

This observance helps us to get a perspective on what is important. Sadie Virginia Smithson of Johnson Falls, West Virginia, grew up on the wrong side of town. She never found herself with the "in" group of her community. In desperation in the early 1900s she made a trip to Europe with money she had earned as a seamstress. She felt that out of this trip she would become a member of her community's literary league.

During the trip, World War I exploded across the Continent. One day Sadie Virginia Smithson found herself in the middle of a battlefield. After spending a day and night having last prayers with dying men, carrying water to the wounded, writing fleeting letters home, Sadie found her entire value system reconstructed.

On the ship back home, one of her party said, "Well, Sadie, I guess you will now make the literary league."

"It don't matter no more," Sadie replied.

"Doesn't matter? What do you mean?" asked the questioner. Then Sadie related her story. "Well, Sadie, what does matter?" she asked.

Sadie replied, "Nothing except God, doing things for folks, and love."

The observance of these acts of love always stands as a memorial to the love of Christ. It is but a step from here to Christ's memorial of love to us. Soon after this event, Jesus went to the cross. By his death on the cross, he gave us a final statement of the extravagance of love. Love is so extravagant in its expression that even the Son of God went to his death in love for us.

From out of the crowd came Mary of Bethany to show her love to Jesus in an act of extravagant love. This reminds us that love is always costly. But it also inspires us to show our love to that one who has shown his love so mightily to us.

Part IV
The Crowd at the Cross

Crucified on the public garbage dump Jesus did not die alone. There was a crowd at his crucifixion. Unable to suffer in private Jesus touched people in his death. The events surrounding the crucifixion show Christ dealing with people in the crowd even to the very end of his life.

13

Priests: The Resisting of Reality

Do you remember the play and movie, *Harvey?* Elwood P. Dowd lived in a dream world. He had a faithful friend and companion, Harvey, a six-foot-tall rabbit. The play revolved around the attempts of his family to get Elwood P. Dowd to come down to earth and to face reality. He resisted. He found life much more enjoyable and exciting when he lived in his dream world with his rabbit friend Harvey.

Throughout history people have resisted reality. Many of us spend a lot of time hoping for a condition that will never exist, yearning for a time that can never return, or glamorizing days that were really quite simple and ordinary. This is not quite facing the realities of life. But there are times when it is more comfortable and convenient to resist reality.

Fantasizing happens in our spiritual lives too. Sometimes we resist spiritual reality. In the crowd around the cross of Jesus Christ, this attitude is represented by and personified in the priests. They had resisted reality. True, they had engineered the crucifixion of Jesus of Nazareth. But in the very act of bringing about Jesus' death, they had resisted the reality of his life and mission.

A familiar black spiritual asks, "Were you there when they crucified my Lord?" We were not there physically; but as we examine some of the faces that ring the cross during the execution of Jesus, we can see some of the same attitudes reflected in our lives.

Let's begin with the priests. Their reaction to Jesus drove him to the cross. Religiously, we could say that the priests resisted reality. They could neither understand nor accept that God had a new way of dealing directly with people. Their whole lives had been wrapped up in acting as intermediaries between God and the people. To assert that people could directly approach God would undercut their position. To assert that people could relate to God by love and obedience rather than sacrifice and religious observances would destroy their power.

From the trial of Jesus before Caiaphas the high priest, we are able to see the priests in their act of resisting reality (Matt. 26:57-68). Jesus had come into the world as the promised Redeemer of humankind, the promised Deliverer from sin. The priests could not accept this reality. The priests stand out in the crowd at the cross as those who resisted reality.

Distinction

As we look at these priests who had orchestrated the arrest and the trial of Jesus, we can make the distinction between being religious and being Christian.

The priests were religious. They made sure that religion kept going. In Jesus' time, there were approximately one hundred thousand priests. There were so many of them that they were divided into twenty-four courses that served in the Temple two weeks during the year. The only time all the priests served was during the three major feasts: Passover, Pentecost, and Tabernacles.

The only qualification for the priesthood was unbroken physical descent from Aaron. There were no spiritual qualifications or no moral qualifications. If a man did not descend from Aaron, nothing could make him a priest. If he did descend from Aaron, nothing could keep him from being a priest. A few physical defects could keep a man from serving, but nothing could disqualify him from being counted as a priest.

The priesthood was a position of privilege. The amount of meat consumed in a burnt offering was very small. The priests received for their own use what was not consumed. The peace offering was an exception, but even then they received the choice portions. This meat could be eaten in any clean place which allowed it to be distributed to the nonofficiating priests also and eaten in their homes. The priests received the proceeds from the offerings of firstfruits which were presented to God. This was produce which they could use. A special Temple offering was given for the upkeep of the priests. In a very poor country, these priests were persons of privilege.

The priesthood was also a position of power. The priest stood between God and man. He literally had the power to bring a person into the presence of God or to bar him from the presence of God.

Then Jesus came.

Jesus was not a priest. Jesus was not a recognized, trained teacher. The things that Jesus taught ran counter to the priests' teaching and position. Jesus taught the kingdom of God rather than the Temple; he taught the sacrifice of self rather than the sacrifice of animals; he taught the relationship to God by faith rather than dependence on the sacrificial system; he taught love rather than law. Clearly, if Jesus were right, the priests were wrong.

We still struggle with the distinction between merely being religious and being Christian.

Dietrich Bonhoeffer, the German Christian martyr during World War II, wrote of a "religionless Christianity." He described it as a Christian faith that would follow Christ without the structures of religion. Bonhoeffer likely was looking toward a time when the structures could not continue. While it is true that structures sometimes get in the way of faith and Christ is sometimes lost in the concepts, to follow Christ is not such an individual matter that it has no corporate meaning. We are not Christians in isolation. We are Christians in community with other Christians who seek to follow Christ. We must have a Christ-centered faith.

Some people solve the problem by lapsing into legalism. They want easy answers and neat solutions. Religion then is decided by a list of do's and don'ts. The questions are already answered because a rule has already been established. Modern legalism resists the reality of the liberating spirit of Christ who leads us into decisions based on scriptural truths, the nature of God, and the leadership of the Holy Spirit.

Complex problems of living for Christ in a complicated, confusing world do not lend themselves to easy answers. But this does not become a do-your-own-thing approach to Christian faith. There are some guidelines; there are some benchmarks. We always have the principles of the Scripture and the reality of Christ himself. The Holy Spirit exerts leadership to which we must respond.

Being Christian is not simply a matter of being sincere. The priests were sincere in what they believed. But as we examine the distinction between the priests and Jesus, we are aware that the priests were sincerely wrong.

The challenge is to follow Christ. We must commit ourselves to Christ in faith. Several years ago an unusual incident occurred. Three young men from out of state were baptized in the First Southern Baptist Church, Del City, Oklahoma, after professing faith in Christ. That was not unusual. What was unusual was that these three university students had come to Oklahoma to spend the summer selling Bibles. Even though they had gone to church a lot, they had never been to an evangelistic church like that one. They had been religious, but they had not been Christian.

Determination

When our position is called into question, we usually increase our determination. We work harder and push more rather than examining the position to see if it is correct.

The priests did that too. They plotted to kill Jesus. They were determined to have their way. In order to have their way, they had to do away with Jesus. That they were willing to do. With increased determination, they went after Jesus.

The plot thickened. The priests understood Jesus' condemnation of them. They were outraged at the raising of Lazarus from the dead and determined then that Jesus must die. They resented the welcome Jesus received when he had entered Jerusalem. They were unhappy with the cleansing of the Temple.

Judas went to the priests with his offer to betray Jesus. The priests arranged the arrest of Jesus in the garden of Gethsemane.

The trial of Jesus was in the home of Caiaphas the high priest. The priests carried Jesus to Pilate for the official pronouncement of the death sentence, which they could not deliver. From the beginning to end, the priests were involved in the plot that resulted in the death of Jesus.

The priests were determined to bring about the death of Jesus; they plotted, connived, bribed, and hired false witnesses. Why can't we be as determined to do good for the Savior?

The priests had a determination for the extermination of an individual. We need a similar determination for the salvation of individuals. This determination would cause us to carry out Christian mission and carry on Christian witness. This determination would convince us that taking care of a person means bringing him to faith in Christ, not eliminating him from life on the earth.

The institution of the priesthood was what the priests wanted to save. They were determined to do it. Others have been determinated to save Christian institutions. In June, 1862, The Southern Baptist Theological Seminary was suspended after the close of its third session due to the Civil War. Early in the summer of 1865, the faculty met to consider the possibility of beginning work again in October. The picture was dark. The South was prostrate. The churches were weak. The school had no financial resources. Many of the young people who would have been students were killed in the war. Some Southern Baptists even talked of not reopening the seminary. The four faculty members met and prayed. John A. Broadus said, "Gentlemen, suppose we quietly agree that the seminary may die, but we'll die first." With that kind of determination, the seminary lived. With that kind of determination, we can serve Christ. That is determination for good.

Decision

The priests came to a decision: Jesus had to die. In the garden of Gethsemane, while in prayer with his disciples, Jesus was arrested. The charges against him were twofold: religious and political. These are two emotion-charged areas of life.

The religious charge centered in the institution of the priesthood. Many witnesses were brought before the high priest, who served as both judge and prosecutor. But Jewish law demanded that two witnesses had to agree in any kind of testimony against a person. The priests could not get their witnesses to agree. Finally two witnesses agreed that Jesus had said that he could destroy the Temple and rebuild it in three days. That, of course, is not what Jesus meant by the statement. He had reference to his resurrection following his death. But they interpreted it literally as referring to the Temple in Jerusalem. Were the Temple destroyed the priests would be out of business.

Then the high priest asked Jesus directly if he were the Christ, the Son of God. Jesus did not deny it, but neither did he answer directly. Instead, he turned the question on the questioner. Jesus replied that the high priest had said that. And the high priest took that as an admission that Jesus said he was the Son of God, the Messiah. That is the way we understand it too. Jesus is the Son of God. He is our Deliverer from sin. He is the Promised One who brings the salvation of God to those who accept him in faith. To the high priest, this was blasphemy. For one to claim messiahship was a blasphemous statement. In addition, their minds were already made up. Nothing that Jesus could have said or not said would have changed their minds about him so blind were they to his truth. The religious charge was blasphemy: he would destroy the Temple; he had claimed messiahship.

The political charge had to come from the Romans. The Jewish leaders could find Jesus guilty of breaking their law, but they could not pronounce the death sentence. They needed the Romans for that. So the charge they trumped up had to do with kingship. They told the Romans that Jesus had claimed to be king. While the Romans allowed a great deal of freedom in local rule, they did not allow claimants to kingship to run around freely. This would put such a person in direct confrontation with the Caesar.

Interestingly, the very claim the priests used to convict Jesus religiously was also used to convict him politically. In the trials they made the concept of kingship/messiahship the issue, even though they mean vastly different things.

Today the situation is now reversed. Jesus is not on trial. His position has been clarified and confirmed. He is the Son of God. He is the Lord of life. He is the one who leads the people of God. He does not stand on trial before us—we stand on trial before him. The editor of the newspaper at Harrisburg, Pennsylvania, was not very impressed with the address given by the president of the United States at the dedication of the National Cemetery at nearby Gettysburg. In fact, in reporting the ceremonies he said that the silly remarks of the president should be ignored. The "veil of oblivion" should be dropped on them, he asserted, and they should never be heard or considered again. But that editor was wrong about Abraham Lincoln's Gettysburg Address. The address was not on trial before the editor; he was on trial before it.

We must make a decision about Jesus Christ. Since we are on trial before him, a definite decision is necessary. The priests made the decision that Jesus had to die when he was on trial before them. They had resisted reality. Now each one of us must make a definite decision. What will that decision be? The question is not, Is this the Christ? but, What will you do with Jesus?

The priests were very conspicuous in the crowd at the cross. They resisted the reality of Jesus Christ and engineered his death. How tragic it would be for people in this day to crowd around the cross of Christ and repeat the error of resisting the reality of his message and mission on the earth.

14

Simon of Cyrene: The Involvement of Bystanders

The stabbing death of a New York City woman named Kitty Genovese has become a modern legend. Stabbed in the courtyard of her apartment building, she was then dragged into the hallway. After her death, thirty-nine persons said they had seen it but did nothing because they "did not want to get involved."

A biblical story that illustrates the same truth is the parable of the good Samaritan. Both a priest and a Levite passed by on the other side of the man who had been beaten, robbed, and left for dead on the road from Jerusalem to Jericho. Among other reasons, they passed him by because they did not want to get involved.

The experience of Simon of Cyrene was different. Probably he did not want to get involved in the crucifixion of Jesus, but he was forced by the Roman soldiers. He was a man who one moment was totally unknown and the next moment was thrust into immortality through something he really did not want to do and possibly did not understand. Simon was just one of the crowd along the route to the crucifixion when, suddenly from out of the crowd, he became a part of the crucifixion event.

We know very little about Simon of Cyrene. Cyrene is in North Africa. There was a very large Jewish colony there. Whether Simon was a Jew of the Dispersion who lived in Cyrene or a dark-skinned native of Cyrene who had become a Jewish proselyte is not known. At any rate, Simon of Cyrene had come to Jerusalem for the Passover and got caught up in the drama of the crucifixion.

One of the records of the event is in Mark 15:21. Mark seems to indicate that Simon had just come into town. Possibly he had saved for years for that day. His day was ruined. Or was it?

SIMON OF CYRENE

In the crowd at the cross was one man who had carried that cross to the place of execution. Whether Simon carried the cross by choice or by chance is not real clear. The Romans had the authority to impress people for service. Possibly Simon looked like a person who could carry a load well, and the Roman soldiers picked him at random for this task. Or he could have said something to the soldiers that caused them to draft him for the unpleasant job. Possibly, they looked across the crowd for one who would shoulder the load for Jesus and Simon indicated that he would do it if they asked him. Whatever the circumstances that led to his hefting the beam and carrying it for Christ, Simon was a bystander who got caught up in the crucifixion.

Compulsion

When bystanders become involved, we have to consider compulsion. Can there even be such a thing as a bystander to the crucifixion? Simon was compelled to carry the cross of Jesus Christ to the execution place.

We are compelled to fix our attention on what happened to Jesus. The crucifixion has a compulsion about it that no one can escape.

Jerusalem was crowded that day. Maybe Simon just walked over to see what was happening when the Roman soldier tapped him on the shoulder. Conceivably, he was just passing through the city on his way to somewhere else when he was compelled by the crucifixion of Jesus to become involved in it. The crucifixion of Jesus is not something that is easily ignored. All of us are compelled to consider it. If a person stops to consider the reason for Easter, he is compelled to consider Christ.

The form of the cross can be seen in many areas of life. When one looks at a six-panel door, he may be reminded of the cross. The cross pieces in some windows may remind us of the cross of Christ. Seeing a gnarled tree may remind some of Gethsemane and the crucifixion. The cross has a compulsion about it.

The compulsion of the cross may cause plans to change. Doubtlessly, Simon had other plans for the day. He did not begin that day with the thought that he would carry Jesus' cross.

But whatever his plans for the day, they were forever changed when he came upon Christ and his cross. The cross has a way of causing plans—and lives—to change.

Ernest Gordon and Peter Funk, in *A Guidebook for the New Christian,* told of a man to whom a friend remarked that he was the most loving person he had ever seen. This man replied that it had not always been that way. He was a loving person because of Christ. When a young man, he was very conscious of power. For that reason he had gone into politics. As a reward, he became president of an industrial firm. One day he was faced with a situation which was beyond his power to deal with or to understand. His wife was killed in an accident. What he had meant nothing to him anymore. His one hope in the whole world was Christ. He turned from the love of power to Christ. He loved Jesus. Jesus Christ changed his whole way of looking at things. The Christ of the cross can change all of life.

Conversion

We have to assume conversion when bystanders become involved. We have to assume that Simon of Cyrene became a Christian, that he committed himself to the Christ whose cross he was committed to carry. Why must we make this assumption?

We must assume that Simon became a Christian because his sons are mentioned by name. In Mark's Gospel the names of Alexander and Rufus, whose father was Simon of Cyrene, are mentioned as though people in the early church would have known them (Mark 15:21). Rufus is again cited in Romans 16:13. There could have been another Rufus, but it is not too much to assume that this Rufus was the son of Simon. In Acts 11:19 we are told that some men from Cyrus and Cyrene went to Antioch to preach. Could Simon have been with them? A list of the leading church members at Antioch in Acts 13:1 includes "Simeon that was called Niger." *Simeon* is another form of Simon. *Niger* means black. Cyrene was in North Africa, and many of the people were dark, perhaps black. The evidence could indicate that Simon of Cyrene was known to the Antioch church as Simeon, nicknamed Niger. The assumption can be made fairly safely that Simon became a believer.

What could have brought Simon to conversion? Again, let us make an assumption. While shouldering the cross of Christ, Simon could have observed the mercy of Christ. That mercy could have brought Simon to conversion.

According to Luke 23:27-33, Jesus immediately began to address the women who grieved over his approaching death. While he was dying on the cross, Simon would have heard Jesus ask God to forgive those who had crucified him. We can imagine that Simon remained for the crucifixion. He may have considered himself responsible since he hauled the cross on which Jesus died.

What do you think Jesus said to Simon while he carried the cross? We have no way of knowing. But it could very well have been a word of mercy. Frederick B. Speakman wrote a dramatic monologue entitled "What the Passenger Told the Captain" *(The Salty Tang)*. Simon is pictured on a ship heading back to Cyrene following the crucifixion and the resurrection. In telling the captain what happened when he carried the cross, Simon said Jesus said he was sorry but that he was carrying more than Simon could know. Then Jesus also said that he was grateful to Simon and to the Father for bringing Simon to help him. Whatever Jesus may have said to Simon could only have impressed him with the mercy, grace, and forgiveness of Christ.

God showed his mercy even to the crucifiers. The wonder of God's love, as expressed in the cross of Christ, is that he forgave even those who participated in the crucifixion of his Son.

During one of the persecutions of the Armenians by the Turks, an Armenian girl and her brother were closely pursued by a Turkish soldier. Trapped at the end of a lane, the soldier killed the brother before his sister's eyes. The sister escaped by leaping over a wall and fleeing into the country. She later became a nurse.

One day a wounded Turkish soldier was brought into the hospital where the young woman worked. She recognized him as the soldier who had killed her brother and had tried to kill her. The soldier's condition was such that the least neglect on the part of the nurse would have cost him his life. But she gave him painstaking and constant care.

As he recovered, the soldier recognized her as the girl whose brother he had killed. He asked her why she had taken such good care of him. He had killed her brother. She said she had a religion that taught her to forgive her enemies.

Commandment

When bystanders become involved, we have to obey a commandment. Simon was commanded to carry Christ's cross. Christ also gives us a command to carry a cross. He said, "If any man will come after me, let him deny himself, and take up his cross, and follow me" (Matt. 16:24).

There is a difference between a cross and a burden. Many people bear a burden and think they are carrying a cross. The cross was for one purpose: death. The Romans had been in Palestine long enough and had executed enough people that those to whom Jesus spoke knew what a cross was. A cross was an instrument of death. Jesus commanded us to carry a cross and not a burden. The willingness to die to self, self-centered living, and selfish desires is what Jesus commands.

No disciple was there to do what a stranger was compelled to do. In the time of Jesus' greatest need and deepest burden, no disciple was there to take up the cross. A stranger had to respond to that command. By this stranger taking up that cross, he has forever been identified with the Christ.

When the commandment to take up our crosses is followed, we become so involved with Christ that we can be identified with him. A Princeton University student once testified that he believed in Jesus because he saw him alive in other people. After having been involved in a campus strike, the student became convinced that even people with noble dreams are too often guided by hate and bent on destruction. Then he met some Christians. They were like him in many ways. One of them had a problem with a boyfriend on drugs. Another one was a very lonely person with a tremendous need for love. They were human beings who had been hurt by the world. Nevertheless, they had a real, unmistakable power in their lives which gave them victory over their problems. They had sincere joy. They were alive and victorious. They had something that he did not have. They said that it was Jesus living in them. He gave them power. The student believed them. So he believed Jesus.

When we become involved with Jesus, we become identified with him. When we carry our crosses, we die to self in order to gain new life through Christ. Upon confessing him as Lord of life, we are then known as Christians. It is impossible to become involved with Christ without becoming identified with him. The very name by which we are known assures that.

We cannot be uninvolved in the world. Life in this world calls for involvement and commitment. Jesus was so involved in our lives and our problems that he went to the cross for us. Let us also take up our crosses that we may live for him in faith. From out of the crowd came one bystander to carry the cross of Christ. He became involved. Christ calls us to involvement with him through faith and obedience.

15

Centurion: The Confession of Christ

In the fourth century, Diocletian carried out one of the most severe persecutions of the early Christians by the Roman state. Diocletian's son-in-law, Galerius, urged him to begin the persecutions and insisted that they be continued. Succeeding Diocletian as emperor of Rome, Galerius continued the persecutions with unabated zeal. Diocletian had his home in Nicomedia. A young Roman army officer, who was a part of the court of Galerius, was impressed by the faith of the Christians in Nicomedia. He asked them the secret of their courage in face of persecution and death. He was told and received instruction in the Christian faith. When the Christians were next examined, he stepped forward and requested Galerius make a note of his name among the Christians.

"Are you mad?" asked Galerius. "Do you wish to throw away your life?"

"I am not mad," the officer replied. "I was mad once, but am now in my right mind."[1] This young Roman army officer was won to faith in Christ by his observation of the death of the Christians.

We are reminded of another who found faith in Christ by watching the death of Christ himself. Crucifixion was all in a day's work for Roman soldiers. They scarcely paid attention to their victims. They had become hardened and calloused in the grim business of killing. However, the centurion who crucified Christ must have felt himself shaken to the very core of his being. Never had he seen anyone die with such calmness and dignity, such poise and self-mastery. In that awful moment, an insight flooded the pagan soul of this tough executioner. It was an insight that eluded even the pious—especially the pious—that this was not just another man dying on the cross. "Truly this was the Son of God" (Matt. 27:54), exclaimed the centurion.

We really do not know how much this centurion knew about Jesus. We are not sure how much of the proceedings he had witnessed. Since he was the equivalent of a platoon sergeant, to whom was entrusted the responsibility of carrying out the crucifixion, we can assume that he had been present for most of the procedure. It would seem likely that he had been present at the trial in the Praetorium. He probably heard Pilate's repeated assertion of the prisoner's innocence and had witnessed Pilate's perturbed reaction on learning that Jesus claimed to be "God's Son." It all came back to him at that dread crisis. At the moment of Jesus' death, the centurion had a tremendous revelation. "Indeed," he exclaimed, "this man *was* righteous; truly he was 'God's Son.' "

That is the purpose of the cross—to reveal God to us. We are to realize that Jesus was, indeed, the Righteous One, the Son of God. We are to be compelled by the cross to the confession that Jesus is the Son of God. The purpose of the cross is for us to confess Christ as our personal Savior.

All in all, the Bible presents a pretty favorable picture of Roman centurions. Those who are presented favorably are Cornelius (Acts 10), an unnamed centurion in Capernaum (Matt. 8:5), the centurion, Julius, who was in charge of Paul on his trip to Rome (Acts 27:1), and the centurion at the cross, named Marcellus by tradition.

Out of the crowd at the cross came the centurion with the confession of Christ: "Truly this was the Son of God" (Matt. 27:54).

Attraction

In the cross is a strange paradox: a man dying a criminal's death, hanging on two beams of wood, naked, tortured, pitilessly taunted by remorseless and exultant enemies, attracts us to himself.

It would seem that the cross would repel us. I doubt that we have really plumbed the awful depths of Calvary and come to terms with its utter degradation, disgrace, and defeat. A cross was the most repulsive spectacle in the ancient world. Cicero, the Roman author, called it a despicable enormity. *Life* magazine devoted an issue to the Christian faith. On the magazine cover was a picture of the Great Werden Crucifix, an eleventh-century masterpiece now in Essen, Germany. Many people were shocked by the grim portrayal of an emaciated, dying Christ who "had no form or comeliness that we should look on Him, and no beauty that we should desire Him."

That the cross should be the supreme means of grace, the strongest link binding God and man together is stranger still. This was not just any cross on Calvary; it was the cross of him who said, "He that hath seen me hath seen the Father" (John 14:9). The very revelation of God is in this One who died on the cross.

To a certain degree the cross offends. The Greeks considered the whole idea of redemptive suffering a folly. To the Jew, a crucified Messiah was scandalous. A free and universal salvation was an attack upon his privileged security. Even with the implied accusation against the life of all men that the cross makes, we are attracted to the cross. Why?

R. E. O. White has pointed out, in *Beneath the Cross of Jesus,* that if all of humanity understands anything, it is suffering, sin, and love. And these three things plainly spell out the message of the cross.

All people know suffering. The suffering of the brave appeals to us. The suffering of the good man appeals most of all. On the cross the only really good man in all history bravely suffered for the sake of others. Calvary speaks unambiguously to a world in pain—suffering can be redemptive!

All people know sin too. The very fact of the cross speaks to everyone's sense of right and wrong. It interprets the world's dark experiences of lust, evil, remorse, and fear. Calvary speaks unmistakably to a world wrestling with evil.

All people know love. Love appeals to the universal loneliness that lies within our secret selves, the longing for friendship adequate to help, able to understand. Deep within us stirs a hunger for divine companionship. To a world in need of love, the cross speaks persuasively of the love of God, a love that would go far for the lives and forgiveness of humanity.

This is the attraction of the cross. All people know and struggle with suffering, sin, and love. In the midst of these, stands the cross. There Christ suffered, as none ever suffered, to show the suffering of God for a world astray. Jesus bore sin as no other ever could, to bring people back to God. He loved as none has ever loved, to show the love of God.

No wonder the upraised Christ draws all men to him. George Young told of his Chinese teacher, Mr. Lu, who was at first disdainful of this strange, foreign tale of a peasant born in a stable. Lu's interest quickened when he studied the Master's teaching, but still he thought Confucius was superior. The parable of the prodigal moved Lu to confess, "I did not know God was like that." But the story of the passion reduced him to silence. The language lesson ended with a whispered, "*Why* did he die like that?" George Young answered in imperfect Chinese, "He died for me—and you." Wrapping his books in his blue cloth, Mr. Lu went out, deeply troubled. He returned the next day a different man, saying, "Mr. Young, I have become a disciple of your Jesus!"[2]

We are attracted to the cross because of what it tells us about suffering, sin, and love.

Application

The revelation of Jesus as the Son of God and the confession of the centurion give vivid application to what Jesus himself had said about the cross. Early in his ministry Jesus had said, "And I, if I be lifted up from the earth, will draw all men unto me" (John 12:32). This is a strange sounding prophecy, even from the Son of God. Knowing the scandal of the cross, we could have understood it better had Jesus said, "I, if I be lifted up from the earth, will drive all men away from me." But that is not what he said. This event applies the teaching of Jesus at this point. At the very moment of his death is the application of his expression of the meaning of his death. By the cross of Christ, people come to know Christ as Savior.

Think of the tender and agonizing story of Peter Abelard, a brilliant and controversial scholar of the twelfth century, and his love for the beautiful Heloise. We cannot understand why it would have hampered Abelard's career if his marriage had been made public or why it was necessary for his beloved to renounce him and enter a convent, but there is no doubt that this experience of sacrificial love spoke to him of the love of God. It especially influenced Abelard's interpretation of the cross. Abelard swept aside the traditional theory of the cross as a penalty paid by Christ to atone for the sins of humanity. The cross, declared Abelard, was God's own act of free grace whereby he took upon himself the burden of our sin and guilt. People see this act of suffering love, and it makes them ashamed of their sins. It awakens their gratitude and releases within them new springs of love that make them new creatures reconciled to God. "I, if I be lifted up from the earth, will draw all men unto me." That is also the theological basis of many of our great hymns.

> When I survey the wondrous cross,
> On which the Prince of glory died,
> My richest gain I count but loss,
> And pour contempt on all my pride.
>
> Isaac Watts

No theology is big enough to contain the whole truth about the cross of Jesus Christ. Even Abelard's so-called, "moral influence" theory falls short when it predicates the "finished" work of God upon our capacity to respond to the cross. We are not thinking of theories, however, but of facts. "I, if I be lifted up from the earth, will draw all men unto me." About this daring saying of the Master, one fact stands out in bold relief: This is no longer theory. It has become history. It has validated itself in terms of human life.

The cross has drawn people to God; it has succeeded where all else has failed. Men and women, who could be indifferent and even hostile to the precepts and the institutions of religion, have surveyed this "wondrous cross on which the Prince of glory died." Their frozen hearts have melted, and their souls cried aloud to God for pardon and grace. The cross draws us to Jesus with the confession—"Truly, this was the Son of God."

Appeal

When we see the attraction of the cross, that it speaks to our own experiences and needs of suffering and sin and love; when we see the application of the cross, that it applies Jesus' own statement that he would draw men to him by his death, we realize that the fact of the cross itself constitutes an appeal. This is the appeal of the love of God to us to come to him in faith and commitment. Against the backdrop of humanity's sin and brutality clearly comes the appeal of God. The centurion heard the appeal, repented of his sin, and made the confession of his faith. The cross appeals to us to do the same thing.

The appeal of the cross is made against the background of our own sin. We realize that the sins that crucified Jesus were the common sins against which we struggle every day, such as, hatred, jealousy, moral cowardice, and betrayal of trust. The preaching of the cross pays sinners no compliments, except, indeed, the supreme compliment that God thinks we are worth saving.

When we look at the cross, we can see something of the length that sin will go. Carried to its ultimate extreme, sin will even crucify ultimate goodness. Sin will even kill the very Son of God. Sin will even clamor that the Light of the world, that Light that can enlighten the heart of every person who comes into the world, should be extinguished. The appeal of the cross to us is made with every knowledge of the extent of our sin.

The appeal of the cross is for each of us to make the confession of the centurion our own confession: "Truly this was the Son of God." In making this confession, we give ourselves in faith to the Son of God, asking for the forgiveness of our sin and the salvation of our lives. One thing is certain—we cannot come to the cross of Christ and not make some response. In his death, the Master sifts the hearts of people. Beneath his cross, the paths divide. Some, repelled, hurry away with scornful smiles, angry frowns, or uneasy minds. Others remain to wonder, to worship, and to pray. Either way, the cross provokes response.

A. Leonard Griffith, in *Beneath the Cross of Jesus,* told of a time when an archbishop of Paris was preaching to a great congregation in Notre Dame. He told the story of three young carefree, worldly, and godless men who wandered into the cathedral one day. Two of the men wagered the third that he would not make a bogus confession. He accepted the wager. The priest, who listened, realized what was happening, so when the pretending penitent had finished, he said, "To every confession there is penance. You see the great Crucifix over there? Go to it, kneel down, and repeat three times as you look up into the face of the Crucified, 'All this you did for me, and I don't care a damn!' "

The young man emerged from the confessional box to report what had happened and to claim the wager from his companions. "Oh no," they said, "first complete the penance, and then we will pay the wager."

Walking slowly to the great crucifix, the young man knelt down and looked up into that face with its searching eyes of aggrieved love. Then he began, "All this you did for me, and I . . . " He got no further. Tears flooded his eyes. His heart was torn by the pain of repentance. There his old life ended, and there the new began.

Finishing his sermon, the archbishop said, "I was that young man."[3]

The archbishop's experience was similar to the centurion's. The realization that all that Jesus had done was personally directed to him brought forth a confession of faith in Christ. This can be our experience. When we come to the cross of Christ, there is an appeal. We cannot face the cross and keep from making some kind of response. The response the Lord wants from us is the response of faith. He would want us to be able to say with the depth of personal conviction, "Truly this man was the Son of God." Commit your life to that man who revealed by his cross that he was, indeed, the Son of God who had come to take away the sin of the world.

With the cross there is a tremendous revelation. Against the backdrop of the sinful hearts of people, the cross reveals an attraction. We realize that this instrument of cruelty speaks to us of suffering, sin, and love. We realize also the application—that by the cross of Christ we are drawn to him for faith, forgiveness, and life. We realize that the revelation of the cross also has an appeal. It appeals to each one of us to forsake our sin and ourselves and to commit ourselves in faith to the Christ of the cross.

Notes

1. Herbert B. Workman, *Persecution in the Early Church* (New York and Nashville: The Abingdon Press, 1960 paperback ed.), pp. 25-26.
2. Cited in R.E.O. White, *Beneath the Cross of Jesus* (Grand Rapids: William B. Erdman's Publishing Co., 1959), p. 11.
3. Leonard Griffith, *Beneath the Cross of Jesus* (New York and Nashville: Abingdon Press, 1961), pp. 30-31. Used by permission.

16
The Marys: The Transformation of Tragedy

In Catherine Marshall's novel *Christy,* Miss Alice is the director of the mission school in the mountains of Appalachia. She tells Christy the story of the marriage of her illegitimate daughter to Neil MacNeil, the mountain doctor.

After telling Christy of the circumstances surrounding the birth of the daughter, her upbringing, and her rebellious spirit, Miss Alice concluded by saying: "So they ran off and got married. But I fear there was a flaw at the heart of the marriage—a certain feeling of unworthiness in Margaret. I was never sure of this, but at least once I heard her refer to herself as an 'accident conceived in man's lust.' And since she was discounting God, naturally she had no understanding of some of His greatest miracles: bringing good out of man's treachery and baseness."[1]

God's ability to bring good out of man's treachery and baseness is seen most vividly in the resurrection of Jesus Christ from the dead. The death of Jesus had all the earmarks of tragedy. But on the third day Jesus was raised from the dead and the tragedy was transformed.

Nowhere do we see the completeness of the transformation of tragedy quite so well as in the attitudes of the disciples. They were defeated, depressed, and despairing after the crucifixion. But with the news that Jesus was raised from the dead, they become the men who scattered throughout the Mediterranean world, telling of Christ. They were transformed into the nucleus of the church that turned the world upside down.

One verse in the story of Jesus' Easter night describes the transformation: "Then were the disciples glad, when they saw the Lord" (John 20:20).

But notice who carried the news to the disciples that Jesus had been raised from the dead. Prominent in the account is Mary Magdalene. But she was not alone, according to Luke's Gospel (24:10). When we read the Gospel of John, we get the impression that Mary Magdalene went to the tomb alone. Luke, however, indicates that she was accompanied by Mary, the mother of James, as well as by Joanna. Marys figure prominently in the Gospel accounts. Those who were last at the cross included Mary Magdalene, Mary the mother of Jesus, and the Mary who accompanied Mary Magdalene to the tomb on that first Easter morning. When tragedy was transformed, the people who first knew it and realized were women.

Mary Magdalene was from Magdala, which is located on the shore near the Sea of Galilee on the south end of the plain of Gennesaret. Magdala was known as a wild, immoral town. Jesus cast seven demons out of Mary from Magdala. The Bible never indicates the nature of the demons. Mary is often identified as the sinful woman who washed Jesus' feet (Luke 7:36-50). So most people have assumed that the demons cast from Mary Magdalene were demons of immoral wickedness. Medieval artists pictured her as a penitent sinner. The writers of "Jesus Christ, Superstar" carried that identification along. From the popular, though unbiblical, standpoint Mary Magdalene was a notorious sinner before she met Christ.

Mary Magdalene was the first witness of the resurrection of Jesus from the dead. When she went to the garden in the early morning, she discovered that the tomb was empty. When she first saw Jesus, she thought he was the gardener. After having been the first to see Jesus, she proclaimed to the disciples that he had risen from the dead. Tragedy had been transformed.

Consider, also, Mary the mother of Jesus. Faithful to the end she had been one of the last to leave the cross when Jesus died. Tragedy marked her life in the public execution of Jesus. But with the resurrection, tragedy was transformed.

The Mary who loved Jesus most since she had given him birth and the Mary who loved Jesus because of his grace toward her were both affected by the resurrection. For them, as for us, tragedy was transformed when Jesus rose from the dead. From man's treachery and baseness in putting to death the Son of God, good had come in the defeat of sin and death by his resurrection. What does it take to transform tragedy?

Fact

The one thing that transformed these persons was the fact that Christ was risen. A rumor would not have done it. The tomb was examined and found empty. That was the fact: Jesus had been raised from the dead.

On any visit to the Holy Land, one of the most thrilling spots for the evangelical Christian is the Garden Tomb. A tomb that probably is like the tomb in which Jesus was buried, if it is not the one in which Jesus was buried, is located in a garden. There is a touch of authenticity about it that greatly moves believers. John William Van der Hooven, the warden at the Garden Tomb, in a sermon delivered there, said that the disciples did not take the hint of the resurrection. Jesus' enemies did. Van der Hooven went on to say that the disciples should have taken baskets and a picnic lunch to wait for the resurrection. That, of course, did not happen. The empty tomb was a surprise to the disciples. But the fact before them was that the tomb was empty; Jesus was not there; he was risen!

There is overwhelming evidence of the truth of the resurrection. Thomas Arnold called the resurrection the best attested fact in history. Courts will sometimes use circumstantial evidence to condemn a person to death. We have the testimony of eyewitnesses that Jesus was resurrected.

We know how the story ends. Tragedy was transformed into victory. While visiting in New York City, a Southern Baptist seminary professor took his young son to see the movie *Snow White*. Since it was a matinee performance, the theater was packed with young children. When the wicked witch appeared, the children were terrified. Soon it seemed that the whole audience was in tears. At the height of the confusion, a little girl stood on the seat in the front and began to call loudly for attention. Soon all eyes were drawn to her. She yelled as loudly as possible: "Please, listen to me. My mommy has read me this story many times, and it all comes out all right in the end. Don't be afraid."

Mary had gone to the tomb with fear and the feeling of futility. Then she learned the fact: Jesus was not there; he was alive! Fear was turned into faith; defeat was turned into victory. Tragedy was totally transformed.

Feelings

We cannot help but observe the feelings of those early believers. As we think of some of their feelings, we will recognize that they are some of our own feelings. But we also remember that Christ can deal with them. When tragedy is transformed, we face feelings.

James S. Stewart has suggested that there are at least four emotions that can be identified in the apostolic band. These are despair, shame, fear, and Christ-forsakenness. We are not totally unacquainted with those same feelings.

Despair had to be one of the disciples' feelings. They had cast their lot with the Christ. They had determined that he was the Savior of the world. Then he had been crucified. Their hopes had been shattered. Their dreams had been dashed to the ground.

How often we feel despair. We wonder if the things to which we have given our lives will work out, if the gospel will make an indelible impact on our world. But with the resurrection of Jesus, despair is turned into hope. We remember again that Christ is alive, well, and active in our world. In the end, Christ will be proclaimed as Lord of all.

We, too, face the shame that the disciples felt. They had not behaved admirably in the events that surrounded the crucifixion. They had all forsaken Jesus and fled. Despite the loud boasts that Peter had made, he had denied Jesus. Judas had betrayed him. They had all fled when the going got rough.

We can identify with the feeling of shame; for we, too, have not always conducted ourselves in the best Christian manner. There have been too many times that we have not witnessed or ministered or been good stewards or simply practiced obedience.

But Christ comes to us in our shame to give courage.

Arthur John Gossip told of a young man who served in the battalion with him in World War I. Due to illness, the young man failed in the face of the enemy. The lad was court-martialed and punished. The colonel told Gossip that they would have to show him that they still trusted him or the lad would go to pieces. The colonel never mentioned the incident but treated him with the old friendliness. A few weeks later when they were in a particularly tight spot, the colonel put the young man in command of the very company with whom he had been serving when he made his slip. In a few days' grim fighting, the young man won honor after honor and promotion for gallantry in the field. The boy said to Gossip, "What else could I do? I failed him; and he trusted me." Jesus gives us the kind of trust that colonel had.

Fear is another feeling the disciples had. When Jesus appeared to the disciples in the upper room on the resurrection evening, they had the doors locked for fear of the Jews.

Much of life gives us fear. We are fearful of the future. We are fearful of much in the present. Life is faced with fear more than with faith. The sale of locks, burglar alarms, and protection devices reminds us of the depth of our physical fears, to say nothing of the emotional fears that haunt us. But Jesus gives life. His resurrection removes fear. We do not have to live in fear. We can live by faith because we serve a living Lord.

The worst feeling of all for the disciples was the feeling of Christ-forsakenness. They had lost Christ. Having lost Christ, they had lost life. Having known Christ and the life that he had brought them, could they go on without Christ?

The resurrection assures us, as it assured the disciples, that we have not been forsaken by Christ. Christ defeated death that day. He can help us to defeat any of the foes that we face, even the final foe. Nothing stands before the power of Christ. That power can be known in the human life. That brings hope and strength! Robert Morrison, a missionary pioneer, translated the Bible into Chinese. The Chinese were pleased because with the translation they said they could see Christ as he is. We see Christ as he is: triumphant and victorious. He takes us as we are to transform us into what we can be through his grace and power.

Rather than being forsaken by Christ, we are empowered by him to new levels of living.

Resurrection day the Marys shared with the disciples those feelings, feelings that we have experienced also. But when tragedy is transformed, we face those feelings and know that Christ changes each of them into victory.

Faith

When tragedy is transformed, we live in faith. The disciples saw Jesus, and they were glad. Mary Magdeline saw him first. While she did not immediately recognize him, she did when he spoke to her. We do not see him with our own eyes. But we do accept him by faith. And we live by faith.

We have faith that we serve a living Lord. Jesus is not dead and buried somewhere. When visiting whichever tomb that is supposed to be his tomb, the tomb is empty. Nobody is buried in Jesus' tomb because he has been resurrected. The Lord we serve is alive. He goes before us. He shares life with us.

We have faith that the Living Lord, who is real to us, strengthens us. We do not live our lives in our own strength and by our own power. Jesus shares his strength with us. The strength that could overcome death is the same strength that can help us overcome our greatest needs.

We have faith that, because he was raised from the dead, we shall also be raised with him. Jesus did not remain in his tomb. His followers shall also be resurrected to share life with him eternally. M. E. Dodd was pastor of the First Baptist Church, Shreveport, Louisiana, for nearly forty years. He told of a son of a Baptist pastor. After his father's death, the young man had drifted away from God. When his mother died some years later, he collapsed. Dodd sent the son a telegram which said, "Love, prayers, and sympathy. Read First Thessalonians four thirteen eighteen." The son read the telegram perfunctorily and set it aside. After the funeral, however, as he was going through messages from friends, he came upon Dodd's telegram. Picking up his mother's Bible, he turned to the reference and read it carefully. On the margin was a comment in his mother's own handwriting, "Our hope of heaven."

Later, on a visit to the friend's city, Dodd had occasion to visit the mother's grave. The inscription on the tombstone read

1 Thessalonians 4:13-18
Our Hope of Heaven

The son told Dodd that the message from him had changed his life. It turned him around. It saved him. He was no longer cold, critical, and cynical. His wife had a "new" husband; his daughter had a "new" father; his church had a "new" and faithful member. As we live in faith, Christ makes all of life new.

When Jesus Christ was raised from the dead, tragedy was transformed. Life was given promise and hope. Those who saw him first received that message of hope. From out of the crowd, faithful followers had tragedy totally transformed. Marguerite Higgins was a war correspondent. She received the coveted Pulitzer Prize for international reporting for her coverage of the Korean conflict. She wrote an account of the Fifth Marines which Billy Graham included in *World Aflame*. The Fifth Marines had originally numbered eighteen thousand when they met one hundred thousand Chinese Communists in battle. That particular day was bitterly cold, -42°. The weary, half-frozen soldiers stood around their dirty trucks, eating from tin cans. A huge marine was eating cold beans with his trench knife. His clothes were as stiff as a board. His face, covered with heavy beard, was crusted with mud. Higgins asked him, "If I were God and could grant you anything you wished, what would you most like?" The man stood motionless for a moment. Then he raised his head and replied, "Give me tomorrow." Because tragedy has been transformed, Jesus assures each one of us of tomorrow . . . and tomorrow . . . and tomorrow.

Note

1. From *Christy* by Catherine Marshall. Copyright © 1967 Catherine Marshall LeSourd. Used by permission of McGraw-Hill Book Company, p. 450.

Afterword

It has been said that in every crowd all Jesus saw were faces. He was not so interested in the size of the crowd that he neglected the need of the individual.

As we have seen, throughout his life while walking slowly through the crowds, Jesus ministered to the needs of people. Individuals had personal experiences with him.

This has not ended. The personal relationship with the Christ is still known, experienced, and appreciated by persons in the crowds we meet.

What about you? Has the Christ singled you out of the crowd for his grace? He waits even now to speak to you, to be real to you, and to strengthen you as you stand alone in the crowd.